Desire

Its Role in Practical Reason and the

Explanation of Action

G. F. Schueler

A Bradford Book

The MIT Press

Cambridge, Massachusetts

London, England

This book was set in Sabon by Maple-Vail Book Composition Services

Library of Congress Cataloging-in-Publication Data

Schueler, G. F.
  Desire : its role in practical reason and the explanation of action / G. F. Schueler.
      p.   cm.
  "A Bradford book."
  Includes bibliographical references and index.
  ISBN 978-0-262-19355-9 (hc.: alk paper) -- 978-0-262-52857-3 (pb.)
  1. Intentionality (Philosophy) 2. Desire (Philosophy) I. Title.
B105.I56S37   1995
128'.4—dc20   94-18922
                                                                    CIP

The MIT Press is pleased to keep this title available in print by manufacturing single copies, on demand, via digital printing technology.

Desire

To my father, George F. Schueler, and to the memory of my mother, Edith E. Schueler

Contents

CONTENTS

Preface

The puzzle that started me thinking specifically about the issues this book discusses, about the role of desire in practical reason and the explanation of action, first struck me while I was trying to explain Daniel Dennett's notion of an intentional-stance explanation of action to a class I was teaching in the philosophy of mind. I never felt that my explanation of Dennett's view made much sense of how his view applied to what seems to be the clearest sort of case to which it *should* apply, namely when someone acts on the basis of his or her prior practical deliberation.

By great good luck, at about the same time I was confusedly mulling over what was wrong with my understanding of Dennett's view, I was given a semester free of teaching through the Faculty Scholars Program at the University of New Mexico, an admirable program operated under the sponsorship of the then Provost, Paul Risser. I assume that I was given this free time because the organizers of that program believed that my research was likely to benefit from a semester free of teaching duties, rather than because they had heard reports of the problems inherent in the explanation of Dennett's theory that I had given my class. In any case, that semester proved invaluable not only by allowing me to read and think more about the problems discussed below but also by putting me in contact on a regular basis with four sympathetic colleagues outside philosophy who kept, very gently and politely, trying to get me to explain in detail the problem that was puzzling me: Bruce Boling, Mary Harris, Charles McClelland, and Rob Schwartz. The paper I read to them at the end of that semester as part of our joint attempt to explain our work to each other has now been revised beyond all recognition (they will probably be much relieved to know). This book is the outcome, I hope somewhat less confused than that paper was, of the project that really started that semester.

Most of the writing of first draft of this book was done while I was on sabbatical in Oxford during the 1991/1992 academic year, a circumstance made possible by the enlightened sabbatical policy of the Regents of the University of New Mexico. During that time a number of friends and colleagues helped in all sorts of ways to make our stay in England pleasant. These varied from helping my family and me to find a place to live, through allowing me to use a laser printer for rough drafts of the work as it took shape, to loaning us a coffee maker, a radio, and a minivan. Vašek and Andrea Lochmann, Richard and Alison Michlethwaite, David Pears, David and Lesley Perry, and Tim and Elisabetta Williamson all have my sincere thanks for their help and kindness.

Early drafts of parts of this book benefited from the suggestions and comments of Jil Evans, various members of the Moral Sciences Club of Cambridge University, Charles Taliaferro, Bernard Williams and Nick Zangwill. More recently the manuscript was helped by the criticisms of all or part of it given by Brom Anderson, Gus Blaisdell, Bill Hart, Russell Goodman, Dugald Owen, Robert Reeves, Jim Swindler, John Taber, and Alan Thwaits. Helen Steward gave a late version of the whole manuscript a careful reading and saved me from making numerous errors. Stephen Schiffer's criticisms of the penultimate version of the manuscript, and his suggestions for improving it, resulted in a much clearer and (I hope) better book. Two anonymous readers for the MIT Press also made a great many very helpful comments and suggestions. This book was improved greatly by the efforts of all these people, each of whom has my sincere thanks, though needless to say none of them is responsible for whatever confusions and errors remain. Finally, love and deepest thanks to my family: Karen, Greg, and Jason.

Desire

Introduction

The aim of this book is to try to understand how, and indeed whether, desires can have a role in practical reason and the explanation of intentional action. To that end a rather simple and (I think) obvious distinction is explained in chapter 1 and then put to work in the following chapters. The distinction is that between two senses of the term "desire": On the one side is what might be called the philosophers' sense, in which, as G. E. M. Anscombe (1963, 68) says, "the primitive sign of wanting is trying to get," that is, the sense in which desires are so to speak automatically tied to actions because the term "desire" is understood so broadly as to apply to whatever moves someone to act. On the other side is the more ordinary sense, in which one can do things one has no desire to do, that is, the sense in which one can reflect on one's own desires, try to figure out what one wants, compare one's own desires with the desires of others or the requirements of morals, the law, etiquette or prudence, and in the end, perhaps, even decide that some desires one has, even very strong ones, shouldn't be acted on at all.

The easiest way to see this distinction is simply to focus on a situation where some agent deliberates carefully about what to do in a case where there are lots of actions possible and lots of things to consider, makes some decision in accordance with his or her best judgment, and then acts on the basis of that decision. In such a situation the agent must have wanted to do whatever it was he or she did, since an action of this sort is a paradigm of an intentional action. (I am assuming, of course, that the agent is not ignorant of any relevant descriptions of the actions being considered, not drugged, not being threatened by anyone, etc.) At the same time, however, depending on the agent and the considerations that seemed relevant, it could easily turn out that what moved the agent in the end was not the thought that he or she wanted something or could satisfy some set of desires by some course of action but rather the thought that something was important or worth doing for some reason entirely unconnected to his or her desires. So we need to distinguish the sense of "desire" in which this agent must have wanted to do whatever he or she decided to do, since the act was fully intentional, and the sense of "desire" in which the agent might easily have decided, after thinking about it, to ignore all his or her desires and do what the law required or prudence recommended or morality obliged. In short, the distinction I want here is between the sense of "desire" (or "want") in which it is possible to do something even though one has no desire to do it, and the sense in which this is not possible. This is a distinction that lots of philosophers have noticed without, I will suggest, always carefully maintaining it in their discussions of practical reason and the explanation of action in terms of the agent's desires, with the result that some apparently plausible accounts of these things are not correct.

In particular, the arguments of this book are aimed against two commonly held views, each of which has sometimes been referred to by the phrase "desire/belief reasons." The first, speaking roughly, is that desires are somehow essential in the rational justification of actions, so that, in one version, for instance, if I have no desire whatsoever to do something, then I also couldn't possibly have a good reason to do it. This sort of view, traceable at least to Hume, can seem to provide grounding for a quick and dirty version of moral skepticism. If, to have a reason to do something, I must in some sense have a desire to do it, or something it leads to, then considerations of morality (or justice, etc.) can't by themselves give me reason to act. In fact, according to this form of skepticism, no "objective" considerations can give me reason to act, strictly speaking. I will only have good reason to act as morality (or self-interest or any other objective consideration) dictates if I also have a desire to do so. That is a quick and dirty form of moral skepticism because it purports to sidestep entirely any substantive consideration of the actual dictates of morality. Whatever these turn out to be, they seem vulnerable to this form of what Christine Korsgaard (1986) has called "motivational skepticism."

One defense of this *sort* of connection between desires and justifying reasons (though not the very simple connection just described) is found in Bernard Williams's doctrine of internal reasons (Williams 1979). This is discussed in chapter 2. But there are other versions of much the same thought, i.e., that there must be some strong, perhaps logical, connection between having a good reason to perform an action and wanting to do so. Also seeming to contain this view is, for instance, the doctrine that practical reasoning does or should proceed in accordance with practical syllogisms, which are standardly explained as having one specifically motivational premise. Likewise for the thought that in certain circumstances just wanting something, such as to scratch one's nose, automatically gives one reason to satisfy that desire. Both these latter two views are explored in chapter 3.

The other sort of view that has been referred to by the phrase "desire/belief reasons" is one that purports to give a model for the *explanation* of actions in terms of the agent's

4   desires and beliefs. That is, while the first view sees desires as somehow essential in making actions rational or reasonable (i.e., "justified" in some since of that word), the second sees them as essential to the explanation of actions. No doubt many who hold this second sort of view do so because they are also attracted to the first sort, and vice versa. If one thinks that desires are somehow involved in what makes for rational action and that people are essentially (or even just sometimes) rational, then it will be plausible to hold that we must explain action, or at least rational action, in terms of the agent's desires. Conversely, if one thinks that desires must be involved in the explanation of all intentional actions and that people at least sometimes act for good reasons, then, of course, desires will have to be somehow included in good or justifying reasons.

In this book two versions of this explanatory thesis are considered. In chapter 4, I look at two varieties of the idea that desire/belief explanations of action are essentially causal explanations. The accounts considered there are the well-known one suggested some time ago by Alvin Goldman (1970) and the one recently proposed by Fred Dretske (1988). In chapter 5, I consider the thought that such explanations in terms of desires and beliefs always depend essentially on how the agent in question weighs up (or, if rational, should weigh up) his or her desires. This thought figures importantly in Daniel Dennett's "intentional stance" account of explanations of actions, which is the main doctrine considered in that chapter.

At the heart of many of the arguments attacked in this book is the idea that practical reasoning consists, essentially or ideally, in weighing up one's desires and then figuring out how to satisfy the strongest possible set of them. A version of this idea, defended by Goldman, is discussed in chapter 4. I suspect that it is usually some, perhaps unarticulated, version of this view that stands behind and gives plausibility to much of the argumentation offered in defense of each of the two sorts of views referred to by the phrase "desire/belief reasons." One of the main conclusions of this book is that this idea of practical reason is very difficult to hold unless one conflates the two senses of "desire" mentioned above, the senses distinguished in chapter 1.

Indeed, much of the detailed analysis of the doctrines considered in this book and many of the arguments for and against specific positions depend essentially on this distinction. But though, as I said, this seems to be an obvious distinction, one that numerous philosophers have noticed, and though I try to give reasons for holding it in chapters 1 and 6, there is nothing in either of these chapters, or anywhere else in this book, that looks to me much like an actual proof that this distinction is a valid one, in any serious sense of "proof." Given this circumstance, one might want to understand the arguments against the various theses attacked in chapters 2 through 5 only hypothetically. That is, if the distinction explained in chapter 1 between the two senses of "desire" is a valid one, then the various positions attacked in the course of this book are false or at least in need of amendment in the ways suggested. At least I hope that I have done enough in this book to shift the burden of proof in that direction. If I have, anyone who wants to hold one of the views attacked in chapters 2 through 5 will need to argue that the distinction drawn in chapter 1 between senses of "desire" is in the end not a valid one.

I have tried throughout this book to discuss the views of real philosophers (as I understand them, of course), rather than constructing my own versions of the theories I wanted to question. There are several reasons for this. The main one, perhaps, is just fairness. If some philosopher holds a view that one thinks is mistaken in some way, then it seems only fair to consider the actual view that he or she holds. In addition, there is the practical consideration that virtually all of the views discussed in this book are well-known ones, explained and defended in print by very able philosophers indeed. So there is very little likelihood that any reconstruction of these views that I could do would be clearer than the originals. Both these points, but especially the first, bear particularly on the arguments discussed in this book, since in many cases my claim is that, in the end, the views I am criticizing suffer from a deep ambiguity in terms such as "desire," "want," and their cognates. Stating these views in the terminology I suggest in chapter 1, the terminology I favor, greatly changes these theories, and for the worse. Hence, stating these theories initially as I would want to, rather than as those who hold them do, would be quite unfair to their defenders.

There are, on the other hand, numerous philosophers who have written on the topics discussed in this book and whose views I do not examine here (as a glance at my references will show). Part of the reason for this is just the obvious one that some selection is simply unavoidable. There is no suggestion that the philosophers discussed here are the most important or influential who have written on these topics. Instead, I have focused on contemporary philosophers whose writings have had the most influence on me.

One further caveat: there are numerous philosophical issues and problems, "in the same area" as the ones discussed in this book, that are well enough known and widely enough discussed to have semiofficial names, e.g., various doctrines dealing with the problem of free will such as compatiblism, libertarianism, etc., not to mention the debate between ontological realists and antirealists (about desires and other mental states), and so on. Though occasional mention is made of these and other issues, for the most part I have tried in this book to stick closely to the question of how a clear recognition of the two senses of "desire" explained in chapter 1 affects varieties of the two versions of the desire/belief model of reasons. Even if I knew what to say about the other issues raised by the role of desire in practical reason and the explanation of action, serious discussion of them would have taken the book far off the course of the central argument I wanted to make.

I   *What Are Desires?*

SOME EXAMPLES OF DESIRES

Desires have an important role in practical reason and in the explanation of intentional action, or so at least many philosophers have held. Much of this book will be taken up with examining how and whether either of these things can be so. Before focusing on those issues directly, however, I propose in this chapter to start a bit closer to the beginning by trying to get clear about what exactly desires (or wants) are. And since it is easy to be misled by concentrating on only one sort of desire, it will be useful to begin by listing at least some of the different kinds of desires people can have. I make no claim for the completeness of this list. I intend simply to put a range of cases on the table, so that we can keep them in mind, before beginning any serious philosophical discussion of desire. (In giving this list, I will ignore uses of "want" and "desire" and their cognates where these terms can apply, literally and nonmetaphorically, to things other than sentient beings, e.g., where "want" just means "lack" or perhaps "lack plus need," as when we say the house wants painting.)

One important set of cases of desire, often thought of as paradigm cases I suspect, are hunger, thirst, and the desire to eliminate bodily wastes. (We might want to add

sexual desire to this list as well.) Such desires are ubiqui-
tous and have a very distinctive and characteristic set of
features. Each is connected to a corresponding biological
need or drive.[1] Each has a distinctive kind of "object,"
such as food or water. Each, at least in its more intense
manifestations, has a distinctive and (normally) unmistak-
able phenomenological character. Each comes and goes
more or less in sequence with its associated biological need.
Each has an associated intensity (of its phenomenological
character), which in its mild form is perhaps not unpleasant but in its more extreme form can be quite uncomfortable and in its most extreme form can seem overpowering.
And each is such that its satisfaction is usually pleasurable.

Yet it would be a mistake (one that philosophers have
not always avoided) to think about desire with only these
cases in mind. Not all desires contain all these features,
and some desires contain features that these desires do not.
Genuine cravings, such as the craving for chocolate or for
tobacco, though they often seem to have a biological basis
and may have a distinctive phenomenological character,
don't seem connected to needs in the way, say, hunger and
thirst are. I might need chocolate to satisfy my craving for
it, but I need food to continue to exist. Perhaps for this
reason, it is not so plausible to think that the intensity of
such cravings can actually be overpowering. Compare, say,
the desire (and need) to get to a bathroom with the craving
for chocolate, a craving that might be triggered, for instance, by catching its aroma in the air. Such a craving has
a certain phenomenological character and intensity, but it
seems harder to imagine it as overpowering. (Though presumably to someone in the grip of an addiction, to tobacco,
say, the craving sometimes does seem so.)

Toward the far end of this particular scale are desires
that at least often get called cravings but don't seem to have
much of a distinctive phenomenological character at all, at

least in the way hunger, thirst, and the craving for tobacco do. People sometimes speak of having a craving to see a Cary Grant movie or to go horseback riding. Here the idea of intensity also seems only questionably applicable the further along this scale we go. At the far end, intensity seems to shrink down to little more than "off or on." At this point these supposed cravings, if this is what they are, shade over into such desires as my desire to visit my sister and her family next summer. My desire to visit my sister is a genuine desire, which I might have or lack, but it is not a craving, I would say, even in the way a craving to see a Cary Grant movie is, let alone in the way a craving for sweets is.

What is the difference? For one thing, there seems to be no phenomenological character at all associated with my desire to see my sister and her family next summer. It still makes sense to speak of something like the intensity of this desire, if by this we mean that there is a difference between my very much wanting to see them and only "sort of" wanting to see them. Perhaps this can be best spelled out by reference to what I am willing to do or forgo in order to see them. But here intensity, that is, what we mean by referring to the intensity of hunger or thirst, seems completely severed from the phenomenological character of this desire (since there doesn't seem to be any such character). Nor does my desire to see my sister and her family next summer have many of the other features of the desires listed above. It is not in any obvious way based on a biological need. There is no "thing" (or kind of thing) that could be its object, as food might be thought to be the object of hunger. It is neither pleasurable nor uncomfortable to have this desire. And it is not automatically or typically pleasurable to satisfy it, at least not in the way in which it is automatically or typically pleasurable to eat when one is hungry or to drink when one is thirsty. Drinking when one is thirsty is automatically or typically pleasurable because even if what one is drinking is completely tasteless or even has an unpleasant taste, the act of drinking alleviates the discomfort involved in being thirsty, at least in those cases where the thirst is intense. (This is a topic that I will take up in greater detail in chapter 3.) But there is no analogous discomfort involved in my wanting, even wanting very much, to see my sister and her family next summer. And I might satisfy my desire to see them without in fact getting any enjoyment from my visit at all.

At the same time, my desire to see my sister and her family next summer has other features that at least don't immediately spring to mind as features of desire when one is thinking only of such desires as hunger and thirst. For one thing, this desire lends itself to, or perhaps even requires, the thought that desires are what have come to be called "propositional attitudes," with propositional or sentencelike contents, that is, to the thought that the correct form of desire sentences is "*s* desires (or maybe wants) that *p*." If we focus just on hunger, say, it might seem plausible to think of a desire as simply a relation between a subject and an "intentional object." So the standard form of sentences describing desires would be "*s* desires (or wants) *x*," where, for hunger, *x* is food. This is in fact not completely plausible even for hunger, since what I really want when I am hungry is *to eat* some food, but in any case, it is very hard to see how we could possibly squeeze a description of my desire to see my sister and her family next summer into a form that only allowed us to understand desires as relations between subjects and intentional objects. So this sort of desire seems to force, or at least lead, us to the idea that the standard or normal form of desire sentences is "*s* desires (or wants) that *p*," i.e., that desires are propositional attitudes.[2] It might still seem possible at this point that at least desires are always for actions of one's own. This would mean that the logical form of desire sentences is really "*s* desires (or wants) to φ" rather than "*s* desires that *p*." But this ignores desires for states of affairs over which I have, or at least believe I have, no control, such as my desire that my favorite team win the championship next season or that the weather clear up before the weekend.[3]

Another difference between desires such as hunger or thirst and my desire to see my sister and her family next summer is that it makes sense, at least, to ask what reason I have for having the latter desire. "Why are you hungry?" can only be, I think, a request for an explanation of how you came to be in the associated physiological state (need for food). This is because it is hard to see how any argument or process of rational deliberation could possibly *convince* one to be hungry. This doesn't seem to make sense. Some argument, I suppose, might convince me *that* I am hungry, i.e., might get me to believe that I am. But it is hard to see how any argument could possibly convince me to *be* hungry.

This is in apparent contrast to my desire to see my sister and her family next summer. It makes sense to understand the question "Why do you want to see them next summer?" as asking what my reason is for wanting to see them next summer, but not as asking how I came to be in the associated physiological state. There is no associated physiological state (at least in the way in which there is for hunger, thirst, etc.). But I might well have been *convinced* to want to see them next summer, and not just to believe that I want to, by some argument. I might have reasoned, for instance, that my sister's children are growing up, that next summer is the only chance I will have to see them for quite awhile, etc. These might be my reasons for wanting to see them next summer.

There are one or two more sorts of desire to mention just to round off this informal list (for which, I repeat, I make no claim of completeness). There are several psychological states that "involve" desires in the sense in which a sentence that asserts the existence of such a state entails that the agent has some specific related desire. Wishes, hopes, and perhaps some fears are like this. If I wish the car would start more easily, then, it would seem, I must want it to start more easily. It is not clear what sense it would make to describe someone as wishing the car would start more easily but not wanting it to (or not caring whether it did). Similarly, if I hope you have a pleasant trip, then I must want you to have a pleasant trip. About fears, though, I am not so sure. Can I be afraid that our team won't win a single game this year without wanting this not to happen, i.e., without wanting it not to be the case that we don't win a single game this year? I am inclined to say no. (But then what of the professional gambler in the betting office who, while wagering a small fortune against me, explains his action by saying, in a tone that indicates long experience in such matters, "I'm afraid that your team won't win a single game this year"? If we say this gambler isn't really expressing genuine fear, then we will have to say this for lots of uses of "afraid" and its cognates.)

Something at least apparently similar happens for intentions and actions (I want to say, though this is a point that I will come back to below). As Nagel (1970, 29) points out, there is a sense of "want" in which if I intentionally drink another cup of your coffee, then it simply follows that I wanted to drink another cup of your coffee. This will be true even if you had to put a gun at my head and threaten to blow my brains out in order to get me to do it. If *I* did it—that is, if, e.g., you didn't have to grab my arm, force the cup into my hand, hold my mouth open, and pour the stuff down my throat—then in this situation, given the alternatives (with your gun at my head, etc.), I wanted to do it.

Similarly, some desires get "generated," so to speak just from my making decisions and forming intentions. Suppose that I have decided this morning to run in the local marathon race this afternoon. I believe, let's further suppose, that I can only do that if I am in the best possible physical condition at the start of the race and I believe that in this climate I can only be in the best possible physical condition at the start of the race if I drink a large amount of water a few hours before it starts. In these circumstances it seems to follow that I want to drink water a few hours before the start of the race. And that will be true even if I somehow know that I won't be thirsty at the time. If someone asks me in these circumstances whether I want to drink some water a few hours before the race starts, my answer will depend on whether I still intend to run in the race, not on whether I predict that I will be thirsty at the time. Needless to say, such a desire, though it has, when the time comes, the same propositional content as thirst ("that I drink some water"), looks very different from the supposedly paradigm desires discussed a few paragraphs above.[4] Its existence seems to depend completely on my decision or intention to run in the race, combined with my knowledge or beliefs about what I need to do to carry out this decision or intention. So it doesn't seem to have a distinctive phenomenological character in the way thirst does.

NAGEL'S "MOTIVATED" AND "UNMOTIVATED" DESIRES

So much for the preliminaries. Nothing depends on any of the details of the examples mentioned so far. The idea, as I said, is just to give us a few different kinds of cases of (and *apparent* facts about) desire to keep in mind for what follows. Let us now face more directly the question of what desires are. The first, crucial point to make is that there is a distinction to be drawn between what Thomas Nagel has called "motivated" and "unmotivated" desires:

> Many desires [Nagel writes], like many beliefs, are *arrived at* by decision and after deliberation. They need not simply assail us, though there are certain desires that do, like the appetites and in certain cases the emotions. . . . The desires which simply come to us are unmotivated though they can be explained. Hunger is produced by lack of food, but is not motivated thereby. A desire to shop for groceries, after discovering nothing appetizing in the refrigerator, is on the other hand motivated by hunger. Rational or motivational explanation is just as much in order for that desire as for the action itself. . . .
>
> If the desire is a motivated one, the explanation of it will be the same as the explanation of [the agent's intentional pursuit of his goal], and it is by no means obvious that a desire must enter into this further explanation. (Nagel 1970, 29)

What exactly is the distinction that Nagel is pointing to here? Unmotivated desires, of which hunger, "the appetites and in certain cases the emotions" are given as examples, are said to "simply assail us" or "simply come to us." Such desires can be explained, as hunger is explained as being produced by lack of food, but such an explanation does not give a motive for having the desire. Motivated desires, in contrast, are "arrived at by decision and after deliberation" and "rational or motivational explanation is just as much in order" for such desires as for whatever action is in question. So for these two kinds of desire there is a difference in how each arrives: unmotivated desires "simply assail us," but motivated desires are arrived at "by decision and after deliberation." And for each kind, there is a corresponding difference in how it is explained: unmotivated desires are "produced" (presumably causally) by states such as lack of food, but motivated desires require rational or motivational explanations.

These two differences are closely connected (but compare Platts 1991, 49). Contrast simple thirst with the example already mentioned of my wanting to drink some water because I have decided that I am going to be running a marathon in a few hours. The latter desire would be a motivated desire in Nagel's terms, the former, thirst, unmotivated. This is to understand Nagel's claim that motivated desires arrive by decision and after deliberation as saying neither that one somehow decides to have such desires (which hardly seems possible in any case) nor that they simply arrive after deliberation (as a desire for a stiff drink might arrive after giving, or hearing, a long lecture). Rather, the idea is that they are there *in virtue of* the deliberation; what explains them is one's having deliberated and decided as one did. My decision to run the marathon this afternoon, combined with my belief that this requires drinking water a few hours before the race, generates (as I will put it), and hence explains, a desire on my part to drink water a few hours before the race, a desire that, as I said, I might therefore have without now being thirsty or thinking that a few hours before the race I will be thirsty.

Below I will try to establish the claim that Nagel's distinction between motivated and unmotivated desires is crucial for understanding what desires are. I will also need to do a bit more work to sharpen up this distinction. Before doing this, however, it is important to clearly separate this distinction between motivated and unmotivated desires from another, equally crucial, point that Nagel makes. In the second of the two paragraphs from which the above quotations were taken, Nagel writes,

The claim that a desire underlies every act is true only if desires are taken to include motivated as well as unmotivated desires, and it is true only in the sense that *whatever* may be the motivation for someone's intentional pursuit of a goal, it becomes in virtue of his pursuit *ipso facto* appropriate to ascribe to him a desire for that goal. (1970, 29)

And a bit later he adds

It may be admitted as trivial that, for example, considerations about my future welfare or about the interests of others cannot motivate me to act without a desire being present at the time of action. *That I have the appropriate desire simply follows from the fact that these considerations motivate me;* if the likelihood that an act will promote my future happiness motivates me to perform it now, then it is appropriate to ascribe to me a desire for my own future happiness. But nothing follows about the role of the desire as a condition contributing to the motivational efficacy of those considerations. It is a necessary condition of their efficacy to be sure, but only a logically necessary condition. It is not necessary either as a contributing influence, or as a causal condition. (Nagel 1970, 29–30, emphasis added)

This point, so far as I can see, is completely distinct from the distinction between motivated and unmotivated desires. The claim "that *whatever* may be the motivation for someone's intentional pursuit of a goal, it becomes in virtue of his pursuit *ipso facto* appropriate to ascribe to him a desire for that goal" (Nagel's entailment point) neither follows from the claim that there are motivated desires (as well as unmotivated ones) nor implies it. It is a completely distinct point (which I will consider in detail in a moment). Not all philosophers who have attempted to explain Nagel's distinction have done so in a way that makes this clear.

Mark Platts, for instance, in discussing Nagel's distinction, says that for one subclass of motivated desires, "a complete account of the presumed desirability of its object will logically make reference, not to the existence of the selfsame desire, but rather to the existence of some *other* desire had by the agent. . . . But, more problematically and more importantly, it is claimed that there is another subclass of motivated desires that are to be accounted for in terms which, shunning reference to other desires, refer only to 'reasons stemming from certain external factors'"

(1991, 50). That is, he distinguishes a subclass of motivated desires that are motivated by other desires from a "problematic" subclass of motivated desires that are supposedly motivated not by other desires but by "reasons." Platts then goes on to sum up Nagel's view, which he also attributes to John McDowell, by saying that for both these philosophers, "the ascription of a member of the problematic subclass of motivated desires is simply consequential upon our taking the agent to act as he does for the reason we cite in explanation of his action" (1991, 52).

But whether or not either Nagel or McDowell holds this view (and so far as I understand them, neither does), there are three quite distinct points being conflated here. There is, first, the claim that for any action, from the fact that the action was performed intentionally, it follows that the agent had a desire to perform it. (This is something that Nagel holds, as I have said, and which I will return to in a moment, but it is a claim entirely different from his distinction between motivated and unmotivated desires.) Second, there is the claim that this entailed desire is always a motivated desire in Nagel's sense. And third, there is the claim that this motivated desire is never itself to be explained by reference to a further, unmotivated desire. So far as I can tell, nothing Nagel says commits him to either of these latter two claims.

In any case, the third claim is clearly false, as one can see by reflecting on any action motivated by an unmotivated desire, such as Nagel's own example of hunger (in the first quotation above). Suppose I am walking home in the late afternoon when I begin to feel quite hungry. Perhaps it is because I forgot to eat lunch today. I reach into my book bag for the apple I remember putting there this morning, pull it out, and eat it as I continue walking along. In this case it follows from the fact that I intentionally ate this apple that I had a desire to eat it. (This is what I am calling the "separate point" Nagel is making.) But my underlying desire here, hunger, is an unmotivated desire in Nagel's terms, not a motivated one. Even if one holds that in a case such as this what directly motivated me to eat the apple, strictly speaking, was not hunger but simply a desire to eat the apple (which desire was itself motivated by hunger, presumably), this desire still won't be a member of what Platts calls the "problematic subclass" of motivated desires, since it clearly has hunger as a motivating factor, not any "reason stemming from certain external factors."

The second claim, that the entailed desire is always a motivated desire in Nagel's sense, is perhaps more plausible, though it seems suspect when we think of cases where there is no opportunity for deliberation or decision at all. If, as I am crossing the street, I suddenly notice a bus bearing down on me at full speed, I will at once acquire, no doubt, a very strong desire to be somewhere else. From the fact that I intentionally get out of the way it follows, as Nagel says, that I wanted to do so. But if, in saying for this reason that I wanted to get out of the way, we are referring to something called "a desire of mine," why wouldn't it just be the unmotivated desire I had to get out of the way, a desire produced in me by seeing the bus in the first place? Still, the "if" in the previous sentence is important, since we will need to consider the possibility that Nagel's entailment point simply does not license a claim that there is anything here called a "desire" or "want" (whether motivated or unmotivated) being referred to at all. This will, I hope, become clearer when we consider the entailment point in more detail.

We will therefore need to return in a moment to the idea "that *whatever* may be the motivation for someone's intentional pursuit of a goal, it becomes in virtue of his pursuit *ipso facto* appropriate to ascribe to him a desire for that goal." The distinction between motivated and unmotivated desires still needs some clarification, however. Nagel's way of introducing this distinction, as I explained it, is in terms of two different ways in which we can come to have desires, and hence two different ways in which our having desires is to be explained. Some desires "simply assail us"; others arrive "by decision and after deliberation." Even without worrying about the details of either of these sorts of explanation, though, it is clear that unless we have some reason for thinking that these are the *only* two ways in which we can come to have desires, we will have no reason to think this distinction exhausts all the possibilities.

This problem by itself is easily solved. The distinction between motivated and unmotivated desires can be made exhaustive if we simply drop Nagel's definition (if such it is) of unmotivated desires as ones that "simply assail us" and instead define unmotivated desires as ones not arrived at by decision and after deliberation (and thus not subject to rational or motivational explanation). This will be to understand unmotivated desires simply as desires that are not motivated desires. Beside logical neatness, this change has the advantage of removing the rather vague talk about (and so leaving open the question of) how such unmotivated desires are to be explained, as well as the advantage of making clear that this may be a pretty heterogeneous class.

There is another, more interesting problem with this distinction, however. I explained Nagel's claim that motivated desires "are *arrived at* by decision and after deliberation" in the light of his other claim, that they are subject to rational or motivational explanation, that is, that one has such a desire *in virtue of* having deliberated in a certain way. The following sort of case would then be another example. Suppose that I decide, while sitting here writing this, to have another cup of coffee. This will involve a certain amount of (not very difficult) planning on my part, since it involves getting up, going to the kitchen, getting the coffee down from the shelf, drawing the water, etc. (This planning may or may not be done explicitly and consciously, depending on how familiar I am with my surroundings, how many times I have done it before, whether any hitches arise, and the like.[5]) It seems to follow that even before I have started to carry out this plan, I *want* to perform the actions it involves (getting the coffee down from the shelf, etc.). As Kant is supposed to have said, "Who wills the ends, wills the means."[6]

So in this kind of situation my desire to perform a certain action (as part of a specific sequence) depends on my actual beliefs about how to carry out my decision. If I had not thought that the coffee was on the shelf, then I would not have wanted to get it down from the shelf. But my desire to perform this action also depends on my having made a *decision,* or at least formed the intention, to get more coffee. Contrast the situation just described with a slightly different one. Suppose that, while sitting here typing this, I realize that I want to have another cup of coffee (the craving for another cup has "simply assailed me," say), without, however, deciding or intending to have one. I think, perhaps, that I have already had too much coffee this morning or that getting another cup right now would break my train of thought. Or perhaps I just sit here for a time considering my desire for another cup of coffee without explicitly deciding whether or not to try to satisfy it. Of course, I still know perfectly well that having another cup of coffee would involve getting up, going into the kitchen, and so on, but it doesn't seem true that I necessarily also *want* (now, right at this moment) to go into the kitchen or to get the coffee down from the shelf. That is, when I merely have a (presumably unmotivated) desire for another cup of coffee, but don't, or don't yet, decide or intend to get one, it doesn't seem to follow that I want to perform the actions involved in getting another cup. But when I decide or intend to have another cup it does seem to follow that I want to perform these actions.[7]

My desire to get the coffee down from the shelf, which I will have here only if I decide (or maybe intend) to get another cup of coffee and believe this action is required for getting another cup, is thus a motivated desire in Nagel's terms. I have it only in virtue of my decision and the accompanying deliberation. So what is the problem? Well, what about my desire to visit my sister and her family next summer? Is this a motivated or an unmotivated desire on Nagel's account as I have developed it (or as he himself explains it, for that matter)? The straightforward answer, I think, is just that this is not a motivated desire (and hence is an unmotivated desire) as I have so far explained this distinction. This desire is not and need not be held in virtue of any decision or deliberation of mine.

But this is an unhappy answer to have to give, since, as I argued above, my desire to visit my sister and her family next summer is interestingly and importantly different from such desires as hunger and thirst, which are paradigm unmotivated desires. I can and do have reasons for wanting to visit my sister and her family next summer in a way in which it makes no sense to say that I have reasons for being hungry or thirsty. So in this case the two criteria of, first, a motivated desire being held in virtue of some decision or deliberation of the agent and, second, of its having a rational or motivational explanation, part company. While both applied to my desire to drink some water a few hours before the race or to get the coffee down from the shelf once I decided to have another cup, only the second applies to my desire to visit my sister and her family next summer.

We might simply decide to live with this result while noting the difference between hunger and thirst on the one side and a desire such as my desire to visit my sister and her family next summer on the other. On the other hand, the terminology of "unmotivated" and "motivated" desires suggests drawing this distinction the other way, between, on the one side, desires that resemble paradigm unmotivated desires such as thirst and, on the other side, both desires that are merely the "creatures" of some intention or decision and the associated beliefs about how to accomplish them, such as my desire to get the coffee off the shelf once I have decided to have another cup, and those that are not generated by any decision or intention but that the agent nevertheless holds for a reason, such as my desire to visit my sister and her family next summer. This will, of course, mean that we need a further bit of terminology to mark these two distinct sorts of motivated desire. So let us call desires like my desire to get the coffee off the shelf, which exist in virtue of some decision or intention of mine and my beliefs about how to carry it out, *intention-generated* motivated desires.

We can then draw the main distinction between motivated and unmotivated desires by saying that a desire is motivated if and only if the agent wants whatever it is that he or she wants for a reason.[8] This allows for motivated desires whether or not the agent makes any decision or engages in any deliberation, as well as, of course, whether or not he or she actually acts on the motivated desire. If I want to visit my sister and her family next summer for the reasons suggested above (her children are growing up, next summer will be one of my few chances to see them, etc.), then, on this new suggested way of distinguishing motivated from unmotivated desires, this will be a motivated desire after all, even if in the end I don't visit them or even try to. So, of course, will be my desire to get the coffee off the shelf when it is generated by my intention to have another cup of coffee and my belief that this is the way to do so. My reason for wanting to get the coffee off the shelf is that I intend to have another cup of coffee.

At the same time this way of drawing this distinction lets us see something that we might otherwise have missed. My desire to visit my sister and her family next summer, though it *can* be held for a reason, might not be. I might simply be assailed by that desire, just as I might be assailed by a craving for coconut. If this happens, then though it is still true that I want to visit them, and even still true perhaps that *there are* reasons for me to want to visit them (reasons of which I might not even be aware), it is not true that I want to visit them for a reason. In such a situation my desire to visit them is unmotivated, not motivated, according to our present, revised way of drawing this distinction. The question is not whether or not there are, perhaps unknown to the agent, reasons for his or her having the desire at issue. The question is whether the agent has this desire specifically for some reason, that is, in Nagel's original terms, the question is whether or not the desire itself is correctly explained by "rational or motivational explanation."

This points up something that may not be immediately obvious from Nagel's own way of explaining the difference between motivated and unmotivated desires. Motivated desires, since they are explained in terms of the agent's reasons for holding them, thus automatically have contents that are intensional (with an "s"). Only as such could they be subject to explanations in terms of the agent's reasons for holding them. This is perhaps clearest if we think of intention-generated motivated desires, such as my desire to get the coffee off the shelf once I have decided to have another cup of coffee. The content of my desire will be "that I get the coffee off the shelf." But from this content and the fact that my getting the coffee off the shelf would be identical with my moving the largest can in the kitchen closer to

Mexico, it certainly doesn't follow that I want to move the largest can in the kitchen closer to Mexico. My reasons for wanting to get the coffee off the shelf would in no way explain my wanting to move the largest can in the kitchen closer to Mexico. But they do explain my wanting to get the coffee off the shelf.

One of the things this means is that Nagel's remark about the possibility that another (perhaps unmotivated) desire "lies behind" any motivated desire can be correct only if we understand it as meaning that another such desire might be among the agent's reasons for holding the motivated desire in question. This will be the case, for instance, when I want to eat the apple in my book bag because I am hungry.

Whether unmotivated desires share this same feature of being intensional with an "s" remains at this point an open question. It might seem difficult to see how they could be propositional attitudes without their propositional content's being intensional. If this is so, then perhaps we should at least be prepared to reconsider the question of whether unmotivated desires are propositional attitudes after all. In any case, if unmotivated desires do have contents that are intensional, it will have to be because of something other than the fact that they are held by the agent for a reason, since (by definition now) they are not.

Before returning to Nagel's other point, let us reconsider, in a bit more detail and in the light of my suggested way of drawing the distinction between motivated and unmotivated desires, the case described above of my jumping out of the way of a bus. I am crossing the street on the way home with the light when, perhaps unwisely, I stoop down to tie my shoe. As I am engaged in this task, I hear shouting, and when I look up, I see a very large bus bearing down on me at high speed. I am engulfed by an absolute wave of fear and, abandoning the shoe tying, I scramble desperately to safety on the opposite curb. Here I take it as obviously true (even if it is a huge understatement to say it) that I wanted to get out of the way of that bus. Likewise, my scrambling to the opposite curb was, if clumsy and undignified, still something I did intentionally. But was my desire to get out of the way of that bus motivated or unmotivated? I said above that it was unmotivated, but maybe this is not so clear. Why isn't this case essentially similar to the case of eating the apple when I was hungry? Just as I could have the hunger without wanting to eat the apple in my book bag, e.g., if I forgot I put an apple there, why couldn't I have the fear without wanting to scramble madly to the curb, e.g., if for some reason I didn't realize that this would save me?

Presumably, the fear that I feel when I first look up and see that bus bearing down on me is, or at least involves, an unmotivated desire, in fact one that seems very close to a paradigm case of an unmotivated desire. It is produced by the sight of the bus approaching, and hence explained by this, but it is not, so to speak, that my "ground" for feeling this fear is that I see that bus approaching. Of course, the fact that the bus is bearing down on me *gives* me grounds to be afraid, just as the weakness of our team's defense gives me grounds to fear that we won't win a single game next year. But in the case of the bus, I would say, my fear (with its attendant feeling of panic, etc.) is *produced* by the sight of the bus, not, so to speak, rationally motivated by it. One might be caused to have very much the same emotion while watching what one perfectly well knows to be a movie of an approaching bus (or, if you have gotten beyond such things, consider a child watching such a movie).

But the question was not about my fear but about my desire to get out of the way of that bus. The fact that my fear is produced by the sight of the bus but is not motivated by it doesn't directly answer the question of whether my desire to get out of the way of the bus is a motivated desire or not. After all, hunger is an unmotivated desire, but the desire it leads me to, the desire to eat the apple in my book bag, is a motivated desire. The answer here, I think, will depend on how we decide to describe the contents, on the one side, of the desire "involved in" my fear and, on the other, of the desire entailed by the fact that I intentionally got out of the way.

It may be that for some similar-looking cases the contents will be quite different. In an adventure story, for instance, the quick-thinking hero might have enough time to notice that he can get out of the way of the bus by pulling a lever that activates a mechanism that lowers a rope, which he can then climb up to safety. Then his desire to pull that lever would be a motivated desire, explained by his fear but not identical to it. But in the case where I must scramble desperately out of the way with no time at all for reflection, it is hard not to think that the desire that moves me isn't the same one that strikes me when I see the bus, i.e., simply a strong felt desire to get out of the way. What moves me in this case is not a desire for which I have reasons but just the (unmotivated) desire to get out of the way, which was produced in me by the sight of the bus.

The distinction between motivated and unmotivated desires is a significant one. It marks a difference in the nature of the explanation required to explain why the agent has the desire in question. Motivated desires are ones that must be explained in terms of the agent's reasons for having them. And as the example of my desire to see my sister and her family next summer shows, we can't tell whether a desire is motivated or unmotivated merely by looking at its propositional content.

Let us return now to Nagel's other point. "That I have the appropriate desire," he says, "simply *follows* from the fact that [the] considerations [in question] motivate me; if the likelihood that an act will promote my future happiness motivates me to perform it now, then it is appropriate to ascribe to me a desire for my own future happiness." This point entails that there are at least two distinct senses (or uses) of the term "desire." To put it metaphorically, there is a fault line that cuts across uses of the term "desire." It is the one created when one asks oneself whether it is possible for someone to intentionally do something that he or she has *no* desire to do. In one sense of "desire," this is simply not possible. This is the sense, marked by Nagel's entailment point, in which it follows, from the fact that an agent intentionally performed some action, that he or she wanted to do whatever it was that action was supposed to achieve.

But in the other perfectly good sense of "desire," there is nothing at all problematic or mysterious about people doing things they have no desire to do, things they don't *want* to do *at all*. I would say, for instance, that I had no desire to attend a meeting at my son's school the other evening. I would much rather have stayed home and read. But I did attend the meeting because I believed I had a responsibility to do so, a responsibility mostly to my son but partly to my community. In this sense of "desire," it is perfectly possible to do things you have no desire to do, and to fail to do things, such as staying home and reading, that you do want to do. So Robert Audi is distinguishing, or at least using, the two senses of "want" that I have in mind here when he says that "for any case in which X does A in order that p but would usually say he did not want p when asked whether he does, we can imagine some context in which he could quite naturally avow a want for *p*" (1973b, 7).

The existence of what I call intention-generated desires makes it easy not to notice these two distinct senses of "desire." If I decide to go to that meeting and believe that to do so I must drive my car to the school before eight, then it follows that I want to drive my car to the school before eight. This is, of course, a desire that I can and presumably will have quite awhile before I actually get into my car. And when I do drive my car to the school before eight, then, according to Nagel's entailment point, it follows that I had a desire to do what I thought this would achieve. But the entailment point is completely general. It says "that *whatever* may be the motivation for someone's intentional pursuit of a goal, it becomes in virtue of his pursuit *ipso facto* appropriate to ascribe to him a desire for that goal." In this case my decision to go to the meeting, and hence to drive there before eight, were motivated by my belief that I had a responsibility to do so. So according to the entailment point, it is appropriate to ascribe to me a desire to achieve my goal, i.e., to do what I have a responsibility to do.

But it would be a mistake to think that the entailment point allows us to conclude that there is some extra object, "a desire to do my duty" or the like, that somehow figures in the explanation of my action or my decision.[9] My going, my decision to go, my motivated desire to drive my car to the school before eight—all are explained by my belief that I have a responsibility to go to the meeting, period. It is a distinct point that because my belief that I have a responsibility to go moved me to go, it is appropriate to ascribe to me a desire to do what I have a responsibility to do. This is clearly very different from the sense of "desire" in which my belief that I have a responsibility to go *contrasts* with my strong desire to stay home and read. So far as this latter sense of "desire" is concerned, there is nothing at all to rule out my intentionally doing things I have no desire to do, or my pursuing goals I have no desire to pursue. Nagel is surely right in thinking that there is a sense of desire in which, as he puts it, "that I have the appropriate desire simply *follows* from the fact that [the] considerations [in question] motivate me." (This is what in the Introduction I called the philosophical sense of "desire," since so many philosophers have taken it as the important sense, or even the only sense, for instance, Audi [1973b].) That is why it is so plausible to say that if I did something intentionally, then I must have wanted to do it. But it would be a serious confusion to think that in saying this, we are referring to any desire in the other, more substantive sense in which hunger or a craving for chocolate are desires.

We can see this distinction most clearly, perhaps, by looking at the sort of practical deliberation I might go through when trying to decide whether to go to the meeting or to stay home and read. On the one side, when I deliberate about what to do, I have (as it seems to me) a positive desire to stay home and read. The book I am reading is interesting; the chair by the fire is comfortable; and so on. On the other side, I have no desire (or at least none that I can detect) to go to the meeting. It involves going out on a cold night, driving to the school, sitting through lots of boring talk, not reading the book I want to read, etc. The only argument for going, I believe, is that parents have a responsibility to attend such meetings and I am a parent. But this argument, I decide, is the stronger one. So I decide in the end to go to the meeting. (Had I come to believe that I didn't have a responsibility to go after all, I would have decided to stay home.)

Notice here that the fact, if it is a fact, that I want to do what I have a responsibility to do, *doesn't (or at least needn't) come into the content of my reasoning at all.* It could well be that I am not aware of this alleged fact. It could even be that at the time I am trying to decide whether to go to the meeting or stay home, *no one* is aware of it. Perhaps it can only be deduced retrospectively, so to speak, from the fact that in situations like this one I give considerations of responsibility a lot of weight in my deliberations. But even if I am aware of a desire to do what I have a responsibility to do, this desire needn't come into my reasoning in this situation. It is not the fact that I *want* to do what I have a responsibility to do that, I believe when I deliberate, gives me reason to go to the meeting (i.e., to do what I have a responsibility to do). It is the fact that I do indeed *have* this responsibility that I believe gives me reason to go. This is what I weigh up when deliberating. (Philippa Foot is, I think, making this same point when she says that in such situations, citing the agent's desire as constituting his reason would give "a false account." "For what happens there is that a man is moved to action by the recognition that he has reason to act. This would be impossible if there were not reasons to be recognized until the agent has been moved" [1978, 149–150].

This difference will come out in the structure of the reasoning. If, as I am supposing, it is the fact that I have a responsibility to go that I regard as giving me reason to go, then it at least makes sense to think that I regard this reason as overriding or exclusionary (Raz's term; see Raz 1975 or Schueler 1979), i.e. that it takes precedence, no matter how much I want to stay home and read. On the other hand, if I simply weigh my desire to do what I have a responsibility to do against my desire to stay home and read, then though one might be stronger than the other, it is hard to see how it could override or exclude it.

That is, in the course of my practical deliberation here and elsewhere, I don't usually weigh up my own desires and then do what I think I have the strongest desire to do.

33   I weigh up (if this is the right phrase) *whatever* seems to
me to provide reasons for or against doing one or another
of the alternatives I think I have. These may include my
own desires or even, in certain cases, be limited to them (as
in the standard philosophy-class example of trying to decide how to spend a pleasant evening: go out for dinner, go
to the movies, or stay home and read. What do I want to
do more, I ask myself). But since I am an adult, I often
think that all sorts of other things provide me with at least
some reason to act: what I am responsible for doing, what
my family or neighbors want me to do, what some moral
or political principles say I should do, etc.

The question here is not whether I am somehow confused or softheaded when I pay attention to things other
than my own desires in my practical reasoning. *The question is how we can even make sense of this description of
my reasoning without using a different sense of "desire"
and "want" than the one in which it is analytic that I want
to do whatever I do for a reason.* For in my practical reasoning as I have described it, what convinces me to go to
the meeting at my son's school is not (what appears to me
as) a *desire* of mine to go or to do what I have a responsibility to do but (what appears to me as) the *fact* that I have
a responsibility to go. Even if I am aware of (or believe)
that I want to do what I have a responsibility to do, and I
may not be, this is not what I regard as giving me reason
to go to the meeting. And it is not what convinces me to
go.

So unless we are prepared to hold that reasoning of
the sort I used always involves some kind of systematic de-
lusion about one's own desires, if we are to make sense of
the content of my deliberation in the situation described
we will have to do so using a sense of "desire" and "want"
in which it *is* possible for me to do things I have no desire
to do. That is, we will have to distinguish the sense of

"desire" in which hunger, thirst, and the rest are desires but, say, moral and political beliefs are not from the sense of "desire" in which it is analytic that if I do something intentionally then I want (or have a desire) to do whatever it was I was trying to achieve. The desires and wants considered in practical deliberation are not and cannot be of this latter sort, since the sense of "desire" in which we consider our own desires when we deliberate is a sense in which we can, after deliberation, decide to do things we have no desire to do (compare Mele 1987).

It should be clear, what I want to claim anyway, that the sense of "desire" that falls on one side of the fault line I have been referring to is merely a kind of placeholder sense. As Philippa Foot puts it, this is "a use of 'desire' which indicates a motivational direction and nothing more. One may compare it with the use of 'want' in 'I want to ϕ' where only intentionality is implied" (1978, 149). If I do something intentionally, then it follows that I wanted to do it. But we should not think that there is some psychological state called a "desire" or "want" thus referred to. There is just whatever moved me to do what I did. It could be a paradigm desire, such as thirst. It could be that I thought what I did was necessary to some involved plan I was carrying out, so that my "desire" was itself motivated (and intention-generated) in Nagel's sense and possibly existed in no other sense. Or it could even be that I was merely doing what I conceived it my responsibility to do or the like. In short, when we say that since someone did something intentionally, he or she must have wanted to do it, the term "want" as used here, if it refers to anything, refers to *whatever* led the agent to perform that action, but this could just as easily be a moral belief as a craving for sweets.

To make this as clear a distinction as possible, I will adopt Donald Davidson's terminology and call desires or wants of this sort "pro attitudes" (Davidson 1980, 3–19).[10] Thus (with a qualification I will explain in a moment) I will regard it as analytic that someone who intentionally performs action *a* under description *d* has a pro attitude toward performing *a* under description *d*. That will allow us to reserve the term "desire" itself for cases where it *is* possible for someone intentionally to perform some action *a* under description *d without* having any desire, in this sense, to perform *a* under description *d*. The terms "desire" and "want," I am claiming, are, when simply used without further explanation, ambiguous between pro attitudes and desires proper, the latter of which will presumably include such things as cravings, urges, wishes, hopes, yens, and the like, as well as at least some motivated desires, but not such things as moral or political beliefs that could appear in practical deliberation as arguing against the dictates of ones urges, cravings, or wishes.

It might be thought that there will never be any cases of pro attitudes without *some* sort of desire proper also present, since any intentional action will at least involve some motivated desire, if only of the intention-generated sort. But this is a mistake, perhaps caused by thinking that all intentional action must be connected with some (perhaps larger) plan or purpose of the agent. This is not so. I might do something just because I think I have a responsibility to do it, say greet a neighbor as she passes me on the street, without there being any further end or purpose to my action (and so without associated beliefs about how to accomplish such an end). In this case, since I do this intentionally, it follows that I want to do it (that is, I have a pro attitude towards doing it). But I have no desire proper to do it, motivated or unmotivated.

It is also worth noticing that an agent need not always intend to do what he or she does intentionally. Consider Michael Bratman's example of intentionally wearing down the soles of his best running shoes during a race, where this is something he does intentionally only because it is a foreseen consequence, but not an intended consequence, of running in the race (Bratman 1987, 123). Carl Ginet, who gives some further examples, makes this point by saying, "In general, side effects of an intended action that the agent *expects* (in the sense that she is aware at the time of choosing the action that she will or might thereby bring them about) need not therefore be effects the agent *intends* to bring about, but they are therefore effects she brings about intentionally" (1990, 76).

In Bratman's example it is not at all obvious that he has a pro attitude toward wearing down the soles of his shoes, but this seems to be because it is reasonably clear that this is not something he *intends* to do either. (It does, of course, seem clear that he need have no proper desire to do it.) So we should understand the claim that if I do something intentionally, it follows that I have a pro attitude toward doing whatever it is I am doing as applying only to things I intend to do. I might put this by saying that when I do something intentionally, it follows that I had a pro attitude toward doing whatever it was, if anything, that I was trying to achieve (but *not* toward things done unintentionally or things done intentionally that nevertheless I did not intend to do or, of course, things I "do" but that are not even actions at all, such as falling asleep during afternoon lectures). A glance at the quotation above from Nagel (1970, 29–30) will show, I think, that this is a plausible way of understanding his claim. (Having noted this qualification, for simplicity of expression I will not usually repeat it when discussing pro attitudes and desires proper. So far as I can tell, nothing in the discussion that follows turns on it.)

It is worth pointing out here that just making this distinction between pro attitudes and desires proper is not enough all by itself to show that pro attitudes are not causes of actions, as some philosophers seem to have held. Don Locke, after giving an account of the difference between pro attitudes and desires proper (though using different labels), goes on to say, "The problem for [pro attitudes] as causes is that once 'desire' is interpreted in the broader, more formal way, they cease to be real existences. . . . [A pro attitude] is not an identifiable something which causes the behavior, in the way that poisons are particular substances which cause illness, and fevers are physiological states which cause high temperatures: the [pro attitude] is simply the tendency to behave in that way, for whatever reason; it is the causing, not the cause" (1982, 243).

But this, I think, moves too fast. It tries to squeeze too much out of this distinction. That an agent intentionally performed some action (under some description) entails that he or she had a pro attitude toward performing the act (so described). This tells us nothing about the role of the pro attitude in explaining the action. In particular, it doesn't tell us that the pro attitude (even if we assume there is some*thing* to be referred to in this way) caused the action. But not telling us that it *is* a cause is not a way of telling us that it is *not* a cause. Nothing is not something. Locke confuses two things: (1) the fact that in saying that an agent had a pro attitude toward doing what he or she did, we do not *thereby* pick out a specific causal or explanatory factor or even kind of factor, which is true, and (2) the claim that at *least* some of the things thus picked out are *not* causal factors, which is a different claim and still open. Some explanations use what might be called inherently causal concepts and thus wear their causal nature on their sleeves, so to speak, e.g., when I explain the destruction of a house by saying that it burned down. Explanations of actions in terms of pro attitudes seem not to be like that (though this is an issue I will return to in chapter

4 below). But it might still turn out that all the (perhaps extremely various) sorts of "things" that lead people to act, and hence justify speaking of pro attitudes toward some goals, are causes of the actions to which they lead.

It could even turn out that pro attitudes, or whatever justifies speaking about pro attitudes, cause actions (perhaps in conjunction with factual beliefs) but that *explanations* of such actions by reference to these pro attitudes are not causal explanations. This is because whether some description of events is an explanation of them depends in large part on how these events are described, whereas whether the events are causally related doesn't depend on this at all. As Colin McGinn, following Davidson (1963), puts it, "The concept of causation is extensional while that of explanation is intensional; or as we might put it, causation is a relation between events howsoever described, but causal explanation relates sentences and so the descriptions under which the events are brought are relevant to the truth-values of an explanation statement" McGinn 1979, 27).

PLATTS'S TAXONOMY OF DESIRES

The question of whether a particular use of "desire" or "want" refers to a pro attitude or to a desire proper turns, as I have said, on the answer to the question of whether it would be possible to perform the action in question without having a desire in the sense used. This leaves what I am calling "pro attitudes" as indicators of "motivational direction and nothing more," as Foot says. But it leaves desires proper as a very heterogeneous looking group. Even when we have made the further distinction, within desires proper, between motivated and unmotivated desires, quite a mixed bag still remains, especially on the unmotivated side of the divide. "Paradigm" desires such as hunger and thirst, as well as cravings, yens, urges, whims, hopes, wishes, and probably a lot more, all need to be sorted out. Whether it is necessary, or even possible, to do this, I am not sure. But before moving on in the next chapter to the idea that desires are justifying reasons for actions, it might be useful to look briefly at an attempt to reduce the confusion.

Mark Platts has recently proposed "a philosophical taxonomy of desire, a philosophical description of different general *kinds* of desire" (1991, 49). And if I understand him, he means by "desire" here what I am calling desire proper. Platts accepts motivated desires as one kind of desire and distinguishes within this class of desires a subclass where a "complete desirability characterization" of the object of desire makes reference to a further desire and another subclass where this is not the case.

Within the class of unmotivated desires, Platts suggests that we first need to distinguish what Stephen Schiffer (1976) calls "reason-providing" or r-p desires from the others.[11] According to Platts,

Such [reason-providing] desires have an essential phenomenological character, being either disagreeable in feeling when not satisfied, agreeable or pleasurable in feeling upon satisfaction or both. Yet more theoretically, any such desire is logically self-referential in the sense that any full specification of the object of desire—any complete desirability characterization of its object—makes logical reference to existence of the very desire itself. Moreover, the way in which that reference is there made serves to explain why it is that this desirability of the object of desire does not "transcend" the existence of that desire: on contemplating a possible world in which he does not have the desire concerned, the agent should see no desirability of this kind in the realization therein of what is his actual object of desire as specified by some incomplete desirability characterization of it. The most familiar cases of desires of this kind are the appetitive. (1991, 73)[12]

The other subclass of unmotivated desires that Platts distinguishes are ones that lack each of these features of reason-providing desires, i.e., they have no "essential phenomenological character," are not self-referential, etc. "Such desires," Platts says, "are those which most invite the thought: *he just wants it*" (1991, 74).

We will need to examine below the nature of Schiffer's "reason-providing desires" (including whether they deserve this title). The question here, however, is whether they can be used to produce a taxonomy of desires in the way Platts thinks. On Platts's account, unmotivated desires come in just two dramatically different flavors, those that have *all* the features Platts attributes to reason-providing desires and those have *none* of those features (aside, that is, from being unmotivated). If this is true, it is a remarkable and puzzling fact, since the features of Platts's class of r-p desires—self-reference, a distinct phenomenological character, a connection to pleasure or discomfort, etc.—seem quite unconnected. So it should seem puzzling why there shouldn't be some unmotivated desires with some of these features, such as a distinct phenomenological character say, but without others, such as self-reference.

In fact, as Platts explains his taxonomy at least, it would appear that there are such unmotivated desires that fit neither of his two subclasses. As Platts explains the self-reference of r-p desires, the idea is that what is desirable to the agent about the object of such a desire is completely exhausted by the fact that he wants it. "On contemplating a possible world in which he does not have the desire concerned," Platts says, "the agent should see no desirability of this kind in the realization therein of what is his actual object of desire" (1991, 73). This would fit, for instance, my craving for chocolate. Chocolate is attractive to me just because I have this craving. In a possible world in which I had no such craving, chocolate (other things being equal) would leave me cold. But then what about paradigm unmotivated desires, such as hunger and thirst?[13]

Platts (1991, 73) gives as an example of an r-p desire having "some distinctive intense thirst for some specific fluid," a phrase that makes one think that he has in mind a craving, such as for mint juleps, say, rather than thirst properly speaking. Thirst is not just a craving for water; it is at least a craving for water that results from one's need for water. There are diseases that make one feel thirsty (i.e., give one a craving for water which craving has the distinctive phenomenological character of thirst) even when one is not "actually thirsty" (i.e., when one is not in need of water). So thirst, though it certainly has a distinctive phenomenological character, is not "self-referential," as Platts explains this feature. In a possible world in which I wasn't thirsty (e.g., because I had no particular desire to drink water which desire had the phenomenological character of thirst), drinking water might still seem desirable to me if I realized that I needed water.

It would be possible to rewrite Platts's proposed taxonomy of desires simply to include, under the class of unmotivated desires, one subclass labeled "r-p desires" and another subclass labeled "others." This would prevent the annoying problem of having desires that fall outside every category. But it would do so at the cost of making the categories completely unilluminating and thus of defeating the main point of a philosophical taxonomy in the first place. A major part of the justification for taking seriously the two distinctions pressed in this chapter, between motivated and unmotivated desires and between pro attitudes and desires proper, rests on the claim that, as we will see below, these distinctions are crucial if we are to understand the role of desires in practical reason and the explanation of behavior.

2

Desires as Justifying Reasons:
Part 1, Internal Reasons

"Desire is the crux of practical reasoning," Dennis Stampe (1987, 381) says, "and around it we turn." In contemporary philosophy of action and ethics, reference is frequently made to "the desire/belief model of reasons" or to "desire/belief reasons." But we need to distinguish two doctrines, both of which are widely accepted: the so-called desire/belief model of *agents'* reasons and the "internal" account of *justifying* reasons, i.e., the idea that justifying reasons for acting must include a desire or other motive of the agent in question. These doctrines are often jointly held, and in fact often not clearly distinguished from each other. So in order to examine them, as we will begin to do in this chapter, we need to start by making clear exactly what each says.

The most straightforward way to begin is probably just to quote the best known versions of each of these doctrines. Here then is Donald Davidson's version of the desire/belief model of action explanation in "Actions, Reasons, and Causes":

C1 R is a primary reason why an agent performed the action A under the description d only if R consists of a pro attitude of the agent towards actions with a certain property, and a belief of the agent that A, under the description d, has that property. (1980, 5)

In the same essay Davidson famously argues for a second claim:

C2   A primary reason for an action is its cause. (1980, 12)

In the essay from which these quotes are taken at least, there is some textual ground for confusion as to whether Davidson intended these two conditions to be both necessary and sufficient for explanations of actions in terms of the agent's reasons (i.e., for what he calls "rationalizations") or only as necessary conditions.[1] For our purposes at the moment, however, it is enough that "the desire/belief model" of explanation include the claim that primary reasons, as described in C1, are at least necessary conditions for explaining actions. Indeed, since we will return to this issue in chapter 4 below, for our purposes in this chapter it is not important whether this model is taken as including the idea that reasons are causes or the idea that the explanation provided is a causal explanation, though no doubt many philosophers who subscribe to this model accept these ideas as part of it. In order not to become entangled (yet) in the issues surrounding these claims, therefore, let us consider at this point only a minimal version of the desire/belief model of explanation, namely, simply the view that a necessary condition for explaining an action is that a primary reason of the sort specified in C1 be given. Anyone who accepts the desire/belief model of action explanation must accept at least this much.[2] This will let us set aside until later the question of whether C2, or something like it, is true, i.e., the question of whether reasons are causes.

What exactly is the internal account of reasons? "Basically, and by definition," Bernard Williams (1979, 102) says, "any model for the internal interpretation must display a relativity of the reason statement to the agent's *subjective motivational set*," which, besides desires proper, "can contain such things as dispositions of evaluation, patterns of emotional reaction, personal loyalties, and various projects, as they may be abstractly called, embodying commitments of the agent" (Williams 1979, 105).

The essential feature of the internal account of reasons is the idea that for someone to have a reason to do something or for there to be a reason for him or her to do something, there has to be a connection to something *already in the agent* that is capable of moving him or her to do that thing (even if, because of lack of knowledge or stronger motives the other way or whatever, he or she is not actually moved). The contrast is with an "external" account of reasons, where the claim is that a justifying reason could derive from something completely outside the agent so that, presumably, even in the ideal case (where there are no countervailing reasons, the agent is completely aware of all the facts, and so on) someone might have a perfectly good reason to do something and yet not be moved in the slightest to do it.[3] Perhaps the clearest way Williams puts the internal account of reasons is this. In discussing sentences of the forms "*A* has reason to ϕ" and "There is a reason for *A* to ϕ," he says that on the "internal interpretation" of these sentences, "the truth of the sentence implies, very roughly, that *A* has some motive which will be served or furthered by his ϕ-ing, and if this turns out not to be so the sentence is false: there is a condition relating to the agent's aims, and if this is not satisfied it is not true to say, on this interpretation, that he has a reason to ϕ" (Williams 1979, 101). Externalism, then, is the view that there is no such entailment, i.e., that sentences of these forms can be true even when A has no motive served or furthered by his ϕ-ing. On such an externalist view, Williams says, "The reason sentence will not be falsified by the absence of an appropriate motive" (1979, 101).

It is easy enough to see why these two doctrines, the desire/belief model of explanation of action and the internal account of reasons, might be confused or run together. Both use the word "desires," broadly understood, as an essential element. Both are about reasons for acting. But the two doctrines are in fact quite different, as I think a careful look at them will make clear. This requires, as a first step, getting our terminology straight.

In discussions of practical reason, philosophers commonly distinguish the reasons that explain someone's action from the reasons that are supposed to justify it. Joseph Raz (1978, 2–4), for instance, argues that we need to distinguish the agent's reason for doing something, which he calls an explaining reason, from good or valid reasons for doing it, which he calls guiding reasons. Similarly, Derek Parfit says,

We must distinguish . . . between two kinds of reason: *explanatory,* and *good.* If someone acts in a certain way, we may know what his reason was. By describing this reason, we explain why this person acted as he did. But we may believe that this reason was a very bad reason. By "reason" I shall mean "good reason." On this use, we would claim that this person had *no* reason for acting as he did. (1984, 118)

This distinction between "the agent's reason," and "a (good) reason" is one that can be seen without difficulty by attention to ordinary language. Once we have seen it, however, it should be clear enough that the desire/belief model of agents' reasons and the internal account of reasons are intended to apply to what are, on the surface, two different senses of "reason." The desire/belief model is about agents' reasons (explanatory reasons), while the internal account of reasons is about what it is to have a good reason (a justifying reason). Whether or not all advocates of these two doctrines always realize this, the two philosophers whose characterizations of these doctrines I used above are themselves quite explicit about it. Davidson begins the essay from which the quotations above about the desire/belief model were taken by asking, "What is the relation between a reason and an action when the reason explains the action by giving the agent's reason for doing what he did?" (1980, 3). And if it is not clear enough from the sentence forms he takes for analysis ("A has a reason to ϕ" and "There is a reason for A to ϕ") that Williams intends the internal account of reasons to be about justifying reasons, he explicitly says, "The internal reasons conception is concerned with the agent's rationality. What we can correctly ascribe to him in a third-personal internal reason statement is also what he can ascribe to himself as a result of deliberation" (Williams 1979, 103).

This point—that the desire/belief model of agents' reasons and the internal account of reasons apply to different senses of "reason"—doesn't by itself constitute any criticism of either doctrine. When we combine this with the two different senses of "desire," pro attitudes and desires proper, distinguished in chapter 1, however, we find, perhaps surprisingly, that there is reason to think that the two doctrines can't be using the same sense of "desire" either. This is because the sense of "desire" necessary to make the desire/belief model plausible as an account of agents' reasons is sufficient to render the internal account of reasons empty as an account of what it is to have a good reason to act because it is sufficient to obliterate any genuine distinction between an internal and an external account of reasons.

As explained above, the minimal version of the desire/belief model of agents' reasons says, roughly, that a necessary condition of something's being an agent's reason for performing some action is that he or she have a desire to perform an action of a certain kind and a belief that this action is of that kind. A glance at C1, however, will show that the actual term Davidson uses is not "desire" but "pro attitude." Of course, Davidson gives a (slightly) different account of the meaning of this term than I have given in chapter 1. But, I want to claim, this doesn't matter, because unless we understand Davidson's term "pro attitude" in such a way that it follows from the fact that someone does something intentionally that he or she has a pro attitude toward doing that thing, which was how it was defined in chapter 1, then even the minimal version of the desire/belief model of agent's reasons is just false. The question to ask here is whether Davidson intends *his* term "pro attitude" to allow that someone might perform an intentional action without having a pro attitude, in his sense, toward performing an action of that kind. That is, the question is whether he intends his term "pro attitude" to cover pro attitudes in the sense explained in chapter 1 above or whether he intends them to be desires proper.[4] This is the crucial difference for the simple reason that if we stick with desires proper, then the desire/belief model of agents' reasons, even in the minimal version given above, is not true.

It is *not* a necessary condition for something to be an agent's reason for performing an action that he or she have a proper desire to perform an action of that kind. It is always possible, as we saw in chapter 1, to do things that one has no desire, in the proper sense, to do. "I have absolutely no desire whatsoever to go to this meeting," I might say to myself as I dutifully trudge off on a sunny Friday afternoon to the last committee meeting of the year. Surely, in this sense of "desire" or "want," it is just flatly true that I do not want to go to the meeting; I have no desire to go. So if the minimal version of the desire/belief model is to be true, it cannot use this (perfectly ordinary) sense of "desire."

Hence what is needed here is an all-encompassing sense of "desire," where it follows from the fact that the action was intentionally performed that the agent had a desire to perform it. This is the defining feature of the pro-attitude sense of "desire" explained in chapter 1, and it is the only one on which the desire/belief model of agents' reasons will work. On any narrower (proper) sense of "desire," where it is possible to do something intentionally without having any desire to do it, the minimal version of the desire/belief model of agents' reasons will not be true. On any such narrower sense of "desire," there will be counterexamples to this model similar to the one just given. (This leaves advocates of this model with the question of just how much actual explanatory power desire/belief explanations can have if they use a pro-attitude sense of "desire." I will return to this issue in chapters 5 and 6.)

Defenders of the desire/belief model of agents' reasons have, I think, been pretty clear on this point, either insisting that they are using the broadest possible sense of "desire" or, if this sense is not broad enough, using a technical term like "pro attitude" to make this clear. Michael Smith, for instance, in the course of defending his version of the desire/belief model of agents reasons (which he calls "the Humean theory of motivation") in terms of the direction of fit of psychological states, writes, "If *desire* is not a suitably broad category of mental state to encompass all those states with the appropriate direction of fit, then the Humean may simply define the term 'pro-attitude' to mean 'psychological state with which the world must fit,' and then claim that motivating reasons are constituted, *inter alia*, by pro-attitudes" (1987, 55). On exactly the same grounds as just explained for Davidson's use of this term, I would argue that unless Smith is using "pro attitude" in the way defined in chapter 1, his view will be open to counterexamples.

In short, the desire/belief model of agents' reasons, if it is to be true, must use a sense of "desire" that is so broad that *any* mental state that actually moves someone to intentionally perform some action counts as a "desire" or pro attitude. Otherwise, there will be counterexamples to even the minimal version of this model. Again, by itself, this point is not an objection to the desire/belief model. It has, however, serious implications for the internal account of reasons. For if the internal account of reasons is taken to use the same all-encompassing sense of "desire" (that is, the pro-attitude sense as explained in chapter 1) that the desire/belief model of agents' reasons *must* use, then the internal account of reasons is either false or empty, depending on whether we read it as giving a sufficient condition for an agent to have a good reason to act or merely a necessary condition.

The internal account of reasons is an account of what it is for an agent to have a reason, that is, a good or valid reason, to do something. Its "internality" comes from the fact that according to this account, a reason, to be a reason at all, must be derived from something in the agent that is capable of moving the agent to perform the action for which it is a reason. If that is not the case, then, as Williams puts it in the passage quoted above, the sentence is false that says that the agent had a reason. What this means is that the internal account of reasons can make no use at all of pro attitudes. That is, pro attitudes cannot possibly be the motivating factors that the internal account claims are required for something actually to be a reason for someone to do something if we want to maintain that there is a genuine difference between an internal and an external account of justifying reasons.

This might seem surprising, but it follows from two of the points already considered, namely that the internal account of reasons is about justifying reasons and that pro attitudes are such that for anything one intentionally does, one must have had a pro attitude toward doing it. An account of justifying reasons will tell us, or claim to tell us, what things or sorts of things give us reason to act. Thus it must, of course, distinguish between the kinds of cases where we have good reason to act as we do and the kinds of cases where our reasons are not so good or even just plain no good at all. If the internal account of reasons is understood as claiming that having a pro attitude toward doing something simply gives one a good reason to do that thing, then it follows at once that no one ever fails to have a good reason for doing anything he or she intentionally does.

If, as the minimal version of the desire/belief model claims (and as is entailed anyway by the meaning I have assigned to the term "pro attitude"), it is a necessary condition of someone's intentionally doing something that he or she have a pro attitude toward doing it, then no one ever acts intentionally without having a pro attitude toward what he or she does. So if the internal account of reasons is understood as claiming that it is *sufficient* for having a good reason to do something that one have a pro attitude toward doing it, then everyone always has some good reason to do anything he or she intentionally does. This seems to be an absurd conclusion, as if, no matter how bad one's reason for acting is, it can never be *completely* worthless.

It might be objected here that it is a misreading of the internal account of reasons to take it as proposing sufficient conditions for someone having a good reason to do something. And whether or not that is true of all versions of this view,[5] it certainly seems true for Williams's version of it. He says only that failure to have the sort of motive in question shows that the sentence ascribing to the agent a reason to perform the action is false. That is, his claim seems really only to be a version of the idea that having such a motive is a necessary condition of having a good reason to perform the action, but not that it is a sufficient condition.

This version of the internal account of reasons, it is true, is not open to the objection just given, even when the motive in question is understood to be a pro attitude. If we take having a pro attitude toward performing some action as merely a necessary condition for having a good reason to perform it, it doesn't follow from the fact that someone intentionally performs some action, and so has a pro attitude toward performing it, that he or she has a good reason to perform it. But a moment's thought will show that this reading of the internal account of reasons can make no more use of pro attitudes than the sufficient-condition version.

After all, according to the desire/belief model of agents' reasons, there is no way of failing to have a pro attitude toward actions one performs intentionally. So if we take the internal account of justifying reasons as saying *merely* that it is a necessary condition of having a good reason to perform some action that one have a pro attitude toward performing it, it is a necessary condition that no one could possibly fail to meet in performing any intentional action. This version of the internal account of reasons, which we might call the "bare minimum" version (not to be confused with what I labeled above as the minimal version of the desire/belief model of *explanatory* reasons), though perhaps not false, is thus pretty obviously empty. It tells us just about as much about what it is to have a good reason to do something as we would find out by being told that it is a necessary condition of having a good reason to act that one exist.

Williams's actual version of the internal account of reasons, as I understand it, goes beyond this bare minimum version by making it a necessary condition of having a good reason to act not just that one have *some* pro attitude toward doing what one does but that one have some, so to speak, deeper "motive which will be served or furthered" by one's action, that is, a motive that is *really* served or furthered. So the problem I am pointing to here is not that this version of the internal-reasons view is *completely* unable to make sense of the idea that people sometimes act intentionally without having good reason for what they do, or fail to do things they in fact have good reason to do. It can make sense of such cases, since according to this view the agent's motive must *actually* be furthered by his or her action if there is to be a genuine reason for so acting.

Williams at one point puts his version of the internalist view by saying, "A has a reason to ϕ only if he could reach the conclusion to ϕ by a sound deliberative route from the motivations he already has" (1989, 2). Someone who made a mistake of fact or reasoning, for instance, by believing he had reason to drink the contents of a glass that contained gasoline because he wanted a gin and tonic and falsely believed that the glass contained gin and tonic (to use Williams's example), would then be mistaken in thinking he had reason act as he planned to (e.g., to drink what was in the glass) even though if he did so act, he would have had a pro attitude toward doing so. In such a situation, according to Williams, "he does not have reason to drink what is in the glass, though he thinks he has." So Williams can allow that such a person could have reason to do something (avoid drinking the contents of the glass) that he can detect no motive in himself to do and, at the same time, no reason to do something that he felt a strong motive to do (drink the stuff). And surely he is right about this. Any account of justifying reasons will have to incorporate such cases.

The problem with the internal account of reasons as Williams explains it is that if it uses a pro-attitude sense of "desire" (or "motive") for the motive that moves the agent, then cases like the one above, that is, where there has been some mistake of fact or logic, are the *only* ones that it will rule out. So, I want to say, there will still be no genuine difference between such an internal account of justifying reasons and an external account because no potential reason that an externalist would want to accept will be ruled out.

It might be thought that this version of the internal account of reasons at least lets us conclude that agents have no reason to perform actions that they have no inclination whatsoever to perform, since if it is a necessary condition of having a reason that one have a pro attitude, then (modus tollens) it is a sufficient condition of *not* having a reason that one fails to have any pro attitude toward performing the action in question. So we could say that a person who cared not a bit about the hungry people in Africa, for instance, had no reason to try to help them, no matter what moralists might say about how much the claims of justice or altruism allegedly give us reason to do so. This would be a substantive, nonempty, conclusion that would distinguish this theory from an external-reasons view, which presumably holds that the plight of such hungry people gives anyone a reason to help them, whether or not he or she cares about them.

The whole problem, however, is that a pro-attitude version of the internal account of reasons does not allow such a conclusion. The fact that I don't *feel* any sympathy for the hungry people in Africa (or more generally, the fact that I can't detect in myself any motive that might lead me to try to help them) in no way shows that I have no *pro attitude* toward helping them, since *anything* that could lead me intentionally to help them, including the most complex Kantian arguments, would thereby demonstrate that I had a pro attitude of the required sort after all. And merely by surveying my emotions, desires, and other internal states (including my evaluative beliefs), we cannot rule out as pro attitudes all the possible philosophical arguments about justice, altruism, etc., that I might read or hear or think up.

One might say that on a pro-attitude reading of the internal-reasons account, one at least has no pro attitude, and so no reason to act, if there is no argument (or whatever) that, if one knew about it or understood it, *would* lead one to act (without making some logical or factual mistake). But this is just empty. An account of justifying reasons, after all, should tell an agent trying to decide what to do which sorts of considerations to weigh up (and perhaps how much weight to give them). But the pro-attitude version of the internal-reasons account can't possibly do that. *Whatever* the agent decides are the most important considerations, and no matter how far these seem to be from things in his or her subjective motivational set (even to the agent doing the deliberating), if the agent acts on them, they become, by this fact alone, things toward which he or she has a pro attitude. So from the point of view of the deliberating agent, the advice to "act on your pro attitudes" would be utterly useless: one can do nothing else.

The internal account of reasons will only have some bite, will only rule out the externalist claim that someone who can detect in himself no motive to justice (say) still can have good reason to act justly, if it understands "motive" here as some sort of what I have called a desire proper. But then the hard question is why rational deliberation should be restricted to reasoning from already existing motives *in this sense,* that is, to reasoning from desires proper. My claim is that the internalist view seems plausible only if we understand "already existing motives" as pro attitudes, that is, as anything that ever moves anyone to act, including the most abstract considerations of justice or duty, and *not* just as desires proper. In other words, it seems plausible only in a form in which it is perfectly compatible with externalism. So the internal account of justifying reasons as Williams explains it is left with a dilemma. If it understands "already existing motives" as what I call pro attitudes, then it is plausible enough, but it is also indistinguishable from externalism, since no motive on which anyone ever acts, no matter how unconnected it appears to be (or is) to the agent's desires proper (or other internal states), will ever get ruled out, assuming no mistakes of fact or logic. Alternatively, if it understands "already existing motives" as desires proper, then it can derive no plausibility from the desire/belief account of explanatory reasons, since according to this theory, there is nothing problematic at all about agents' having reasons to perform actions that they have no proper desire to perform. So any defender of this theory will need to find a completely different sort of argument for accepting it.

At one point Williams appears to take this point more or less head on. "Somebody may say that every rational deliberator is committed to constraints of morality as much as to the requirements of truth or sound reasoning," he says. "But if this is so, then the constraints of morality are part of everybody's [subjective motivational set], and every correct moral reason *will be* an internal reason." That is, the internal-reasons view will become indistinguishable from the external-reasons view, which is what I have been arguing. Williams's reply to this is that there has to be some argument for it. "Someone who claims the constraints of morality are themselves built into the notion of what it is to be a rational deliberator cannot get that conclusion for nothing" merely by asserting it (Williams 1989, 3).

But this shifts the issue completely. The internal-reasons view purports to give an important *restriction* on justifying reasons: roughly, no (existing) motive, no reason. This is much stronger than merely saying that there is a burden of proof on advocates of justice or duty to show how such things provide good reasons to act. It is to say that such things *do not* provide good reason to act, at least unless the agent is somehow already motivated to pursue them. It is certainly true that there is a serious question of how and whether considerations of justice, say, can all by themselves provide anyone with a reason to pursue justice. But this question is no argument for the truth of the view that *only* preexisting motives (desires proper) can possibly give one good reason to act.

THE DISTINCTION BETWEEN JUSTIFYING AND EXPLAINING REASONS

What has gone wrong here? How can it be that two theories that seem superficially to fit together so well (i.e., the minimal version of the desire/belief account of explanatory reasons and the internal theory of good reasons) run into the sorts of problems I have been pointing to? Part of the answer is that we haven't taken seriously enough the difference between answering Davidson's question of how an agent's reason for doing something can explain his or her doing it and answering Williams's question of what it is to have a good reason to do something.

It is clear enough that an agent's reason for doing something may not be a good reason to do it, just as a person's reason for believing something need not be a good reason to believe it. Jill's reason for putting on sunblock (that all her friends do it) may not be a reason for performing this action, just as her reason for believing that sunblock prevents skin cancer (that it looks sort of white and medicinal) is a reason for believing this proposition. So the account we give of how agents' reasons explain the actions for which they are reasons must allow for the possibility (all too common) that an agent's reason for performing some action, while it explains *why* the agent performed that action, is not very good or even totally worthless as a good *reason* for performing it, i.e., as a reason that makes doing it at least minimally rational.

The internal-reasons view, if it is to be interestingly different from an external view of reasons, must hold that agents can sometimes pursue goals or purposes that give them no good reason to act as they do. That is, it must hold that agents can have no good reason for doing what they do, because of some failure other than merely mistakes of fact or logic in reasoning about how to accomplish their goals.

The notion of a pro attitude is, as I have tried to show, a notion specifically constructed to shield the desire/belief model of agents' reasons against counterexamples. This makes it useless for defending the internal account of reasons, since the claim that a necessary condition of having a good reason to do something is that one have a pro attitude toward doing it then becomes, on this meaning of "pro attitude," a condition that no one could ever fail to meet except by making some sort of factual or logical mistake. I might put this point by saying that from the point of view of an agent trying to figure out what he or she has reason to do, the internal-reason claim that one must have a pro attitude toward doing something to have a good or valid reason to do it is of no use at all. No considerations, or potential reasons for acting, will get ruled in or out by this.

Any consideration on which the agent acts will, by this very fact, turn out to count as a pro attitude toward the action it leads to. It follows that if the internal account of reasons, even when understood as only giving necessary conditions for something's being a reason to act, is to have any substantive content that will distinguish it from an external account, it cannot merely claim that what is necessary for having a reason is that the agent have a pro attitude that really is served or furthered by performing the act in question. That is, it cannot make use of the same concept of desire that the desire/belief model of agents' reasons must use.

There are various possible moves that a defender of the internal-reasons account of justifying reasons might make to try to avoid the conclusion that this doctrine is empty. The most obvious one, perhaps, would be simply to hold that it is not pro attitudes but desires proper that are being referred to in this doctrine.[6] Since it is possible to do apparently very sensible things that one has no proper desire to do (as in the example of going to a meeting because one believes one has a responsibility to do so), this change will make it very implausible to say that having a proper desire of some sort is a necessary condition of having a good reason to perform an action.[7] There are simply too many obvious counterexamples. On the other hand, such a change makes it correspondingly more plausible to hold that having some sort of desire proper is a sufficient condition for having a good reason to perform some action. We will examine a plausible version of the view that certain proper desires are sufficient for providing justifying reasons to perform actions when we look below at Stephen Schiffer's idea that there are "reason-providing desires."

Another, perhaps less immediately obvious, way of defending the internal-reasons view of justifying reasons has been suggested by Williams himself (1989). The argument above for thinking that it is empty to hold that a pro attitude is a necessary condition for any justifying reason includes as an essential feature the claim that there is a sharp distinction between explaining and justifying reasons. Without that distinction the very first move made—claiming that the desire/belief model of agents' reasons and the internal-reasons theory of justifying reasons apply to different senses of the term "reason"—becomes suspect, to say the least.

In recent years, however, some philosophers have held, explicitly or implicitly, that the distinction between these two sorts of reason (or uses or senses of "reason"), i.e., explaining and justifying reasons, is misleading or at least shouldn't be taken too seriously. Thus Dennis Stampe, in a recent essay, says,

There is of course the fact that we say that a person "has no reason whatever" for an action when we may mean merely "no good reason"; a person who does something just because he wants to may, indeed, have no good reason, even though he does, to speak literally, have a reason. The statement that something is a reason thus has an associated force of commending it as a basis for action, etc.; but that is not part of the statement's meaning, for such suggestions can readily be cancelled with consistency: "Don't do it. Granted you have a reason to do it, but it's not a good one." (1987, 345–346)

The idea here seems to be that, contrary to what I have claimed and to what Parfit and Raz apparently think, there is really only one kind of reason (or sense or use of "reason") but in some contexts the term "reason" has a commending force, though one that may be cancelled. On this view, when we say that someone "had no reason whatever" for doing as he or she did, we are not speaking literally. What we really mean is only that the person's reason wasn't a good one. He or she may have had a bad reason for doing whatever was done, but bad reasons are still reasons for all that. So Stampe's point here, if I understand it, might be put by saying that there is a different way of reading the data provided by ordinary language. When we say of someone whom we admit to have acted for a reason that he or she had no reason for so acting, this need not be taken to commit us to two kinds of reason. We may simply be cancelling the usual commending force that the term "reason" carries, perhaps in the way I might cancel the usual commending force of "intelligent" were I to say "When I call him intelligent, I don't mean to say that there is anything good about just being intelligent: Hitler was intelligent."

Williams himself has provided an explicit argument, not dependent on the ordinary usage of such terms as "reason," for much the same conclusion. According to Williams,

It must be a mistake simply to separate explanatory and normative reasons. If it is true that A has a reason to ϕ, then it must be possible that he should ϕ for that reason; and if he does act for that reason, then that reason will be the explanation of his acting. So the claim that he has a reason to ϕ—that is, the normative statement: "He has a reason to ϕ"—introduces the possibility of that reason being an explanation; namely, if the agent accepts that claim (more precisely, if he accepts that he has more reason to ϕ than to do anything else). This is a basic connection. (1989, 5)

Unlike Stampe, Williams here seems to accept that there is a distinction in ordinary language between explaining and justifying reasons (the former he calls "explanatory" and the latter "normative"). But he argues that we shouldn't be misled by this distinction, because it covers up a deeper connection, the one contained in the idea of acting for a reason.

If the argument of the first part of this chapter is to stand, then, we will need to examine both Stampe's claim that we can understand ordinary-language uses of "reason" in contexts where we are speaking of reasons for action, without invoking multiple kinds of reasons (or senses or uses of the term "reason"), and Williams's claim that, whatever distinction is contained in ordinary usage, separating explaining and justifying reasons "must be a mistake." Since the issue of whether there is such a distinction implicit in ordinary language is relatively straightforward, I will begin with Stampe. In order not to have to keep writing long parenthetical phrases like the one in the first sentence of this paragraph, I am just going to treat the phrases "different uses of the term 'reason'," "different senses of the term 'reason'," and "different kinds of reasons" as stylistic variants of each other in this discussion. No doubt there are deep issues involved in the question of whether in general it is legitimate to simply interchange a phrase like "kind of x" for "sense of the term 'x'," and either of these for "use of the term 'x'." But if any of those issues make any difference to this topic, I completely fail to see it.

So let's look first at the ordinary-language issue raised by Stampe. Is there any real justification for thinking that there is a distinction in ordinary usage between explaining reasons and justifying reasons? Here are some of the data. Ordinary speech allows at least the following locutions involving the term "reason":

(1) The reason (that) q was that p.

For example, "The reason the tree died was that it became infested with peach borers."

(2) s's reason for a-ing was that p.

For example, "Ralph's reason for leaving early was that he remembered he had another appointment," or "Ralph's reason for believing God exists is that the Bible says so." We might also say, "s a-ed for the reason that p."

(3) There is (a) reason for s to a.

For example, "There is a reason for Ralph to leave early," or "There is a reason for Ralph to think he is overdrawn at the bank."

(4) *s* has (a) reason to *a*.

For example, "Ralph has a reason to leave early," or "Ralph has a reason to fear the chairman will resign."

It would be difficult seriously to deny that (1) here is a quite distinct use from the other three. For one thing, though this use applies to actions, beliefs, and other propositional attitudes (e.g., "The reason Jill went home was that she was getting tired" or "The reason Joan thinks she is late is that this clock is fast" or "The reason Jim hates green beans is that they made him sick once as a child"), it applies equally well to events ("The reason Uncle George fainted was that his blood pressure dropped"). This makes no literal sense for any of the other three uses. For instance it makes no sense to speak of "the tree's reason to die" or to ask whether "the tree has a reason to die."

So (1) seems to be a straightforward explanatory use of "reason." The phrase "the reason (that) *q* [was that *p*]" applies to any explanatory factor that (it is claimed) explains *p*. And here *q* can be virtually anything open to explanation, not just actions or beliefs. So this phrase seems to have essentially the same use as "because." Just as we can say "The reason Ralph left early was that he remembered he had another appointment," we can equally well say "Ralph left early because . . . ." In fact, this type of paraphrase is a good test for whether, in some specific sentence, we have an explanatory sense of "reason."

Use (2) ("*s*'s reason for *a*-ing was that *p*"), though different from (1), is an explaining use according to this test. It differs from (1) because it is restricted to people (or maybe agents) and the things they do, though "things they do" can include having propositional attitudes as well as performing actions. It makes no sense, however, to speak of "the tree's reason for dying" or "Uncle George's reason for fainting" (unless we mean that he fainted on purpose somehow). As with (1), a straightforward paraphrase of "Ralph's reason for leaving early was that he had another appointment" is "Ralph left early because he had another appointment."

A further argument for regarding (2) as an explanatory use of "reason" is this. Strictly speaking, one might say, it can't be that Ralph left early because he had another appointment, since he might have had another appointment but have forgotten it, and so not left. Likewise, he might have thought he had another appointment, and so left early, even if he was mistaken. So really what we should say is not "Ralph left early because he had another appointment" but that he left early because he thought or believed (or knew) he had another appointment. And exactly the same considerations apply to "s's reason for a-ing was that p," as can be seen from what I would say in describing why Ralph left early if I did not want to commit myself to the truth of p. If I thought Ralph's memory had been playing tricks on him of late, I might say not that his reason for leaving early was that he had another meeting but that his reason for leaving early was that he thought or believed he had another meeting.

There is one other thing worth mentioning about (2), though it is not directly connected to my claim that (2), while explanatory, is distinct from (1). Although in the form "s's reason for a-ing was that p" "a" can range over all sorts of propositional attitudes (such as fear, belief, and hope), as well as some intentional actions, it doesn't range over unintentional actions or even over all the things one intentionally does. Suppose, in ringing the doorbell, you also wake the baby. If you intend to ring the doorbell and do intentionally ring it, then presumably there is something called "your reason for ringing the doorbell." But if you woke the baby unintentionally, or indeed woke the baby intentionally but did not intend to do so (because your waking the baby was a foreseen but unintended result of ringing the door bell), there won't be anything called "your reason for waking the baby." If I say "Your reason for waking the baby was so and so," I imply that you intended to do it.

Let us turn now to the question of whether (3) ("There is [a] reason for *s* to *a*") differs from (1) and (2). It is very hard to deny that the use recorded in (3) is distinct from that in (1). In (3) "*s*" is restricted to people, or at least to possible agents, but in (1) there is no such restriction. It makes perfectly good sense to say "The reason the pressure is falling is that there is a storm moving through," but it makes no sense to say "There is a reason for the pressure to fall," as if the pressure were an agent trying to decide whether it would be a good idea to fall. ("There is a reason for the pressure to fall" might be used elliptically in some circumstances, of course, e.g., to express puzzlement that the pressure is not falling when the conditions are such that one thinks it should be. It would then be elliptical for "There is a reason *for us to think* that the pressure will fall.")

But (3) also differs significantly from (2). For one thing, it would be natural to put a term such as "good," "sound," "strong" (or maybe "weak") in front of "reason" as a qualifier in (3) but not in 2). Then too, (2) carries with it the assumption that *s* does indeed *a,* but (3) has no such assumption built in. This is not just because, as I have written it, (2) is in the past tense. "Jill's reason for going to the store is that she is out of coffee" and "Howard's reason for leaving tomorrow will be that he is bored" equally assume that Jill is going to the store and that Howard will indeed be leaving.

It is not at all clear what one would mean by saying "Jill's reason for going to the store is that she is out of coffee, but she isn't going to the store." Even worse would be "Ralph's reason for leaving early was that he remembered he had another appointment, but he did not leave early." But it makes perfectly good sense to say "There was a reason for Ralph to leave early—he remembered he had another appointment—but he did not leave early." (Can one say "Jill's reason for going to the store is that she is out of coffee, but she isn't going because she is expecting an important call"? Maybe. But it is hard to see what this could mean unless it is just an awkward way of saying either "There is a reason for Jill . . . , but . . ." or "Jill's reason for wanting to go is . . . , but . . . ," which are just senses (3) and (2) respectively.)

Exactly parallel considerations argue for distinguishing (4) ("s has [a] reason to a") from (1) and from (2). In fact, in most contexts, (3) and (4) seem to be just stylistic variants of each other. In this case, assuming that (1) is obviously different from the other three, the real issue is whether (2) is sharply distinguished from (3) and (4) in ordinary speech. It seems to me that the considerations already given are more than enough to show that this is so. Yet it is worth focusing on Stampe's claim to the contrary before turning to Williams's argument.

Stampe is thinking of the sort of case where someone does something for a reason (so that we can speak correctly of the reason he or she did it) and yet we also say that he or she had no reason for doing this. His claim is that when we say that the person had no reason here, we are not employing a different sense of "reason" from the one used to say that the person acted for a reason but only cancelling the "commending force" that would ordinarily attach to any use of this term. That is, he is denying that when we speak of an agent's reason for doing something, this use of "reason" is a purely explanatory use with no justifying force.

Of course, there is one perfectly clear sense of "reason," (1) above, in which this term carries no justifying force at all. But I think that in fairness we should just set (1) aside, since it is not really relevant to Stampe's claim. His claim, rather, is just that there is no distinct use of "reason" with only the functions I have assigned to (2), that is, that applies to actions, etc., as (2) does, and has explaining but no justifying functions. And he can hold this without denying that (1) is a distinct use.

But Stampe's example ("Don't do it. Granted you have a reason to do it, but it's not a good one") doesn't show what he wants it to show. One can, in fact I think one must, understand "reason" in this example as involving what I have labeled use (3), that is, a justifying use, which cannot be used to explain. Since, in this example, it is clear that you haven't already done whatever "it" is, there is no question of using an explaining sense of "reason," such as (2). There is nothing yet to explain. So I think the only way to understand this example is as saying that you have some (small or weak) reason to do it but not much of one, which is using only a justifying sense of "reason." (I might use these words, for instance, to try to dissuade you from overreacting to a small but genuine offence. Perhaps you are considering punching out someone who just jumped in front of us while we are waiting in line for tickets, say.) What Stampe needs to support his claim is a case that apparently uses sense (2) but must be understood as involving justification of the action in question—a function I have claimed attaches only to use (3), and (4) if it is really distinct.

Holding that any use of "reason" in use (2) will involve justifying the act in question as well as explaining it (since such a use of "reason" carries a justifying force) will lead to saying that whenever we say someone acts for a reason, that is, whenever we say there is something called one's reason for acting as one does, we are holding the action to be rational or justified, if only very slightly (that is, unless we explicitly cancel the supposed "justifying force" here). The absurdity of such a view is clearest in cases where there is a clear criterion of justification or rationality.

Suppose that I reason as follows: I believe that (a) a Republican is in the White House. I also believe that (b) if Quine is president, then a Republican is in the White House. Thus I conclude that (c) Quine is president. That is, I commit the fallacy of "affirming the consequent." Here *my* reason for believing that Quine is president is that I believe that a Republican is in the White House and I believe that if Quine is president, then a Republican is in the White House. The fact that I believe (a) and (b) *explains* my belief in (c). But it does not give me any *genuine* reason to believe that (c) is true. It doesn't make my belief that (c) is true somehow rational or justified, even slightly (to think so is to think that when there are no other arguments around, even screamingly fallacious arguments become slightly valid and so better than nothing). So someone who is fully aware of this fallacy can say that (a) and (b) are *my* reasons for believing (c) without being committed (by the supposed justifying force of "reason" here) to the absurd view that such reasoning is somehow justified. Yet this is just what someone such as Stampe who thinks use (2) has a justifying force will have to deny. (If you still find yourself inclined to think that this fallacious piece of reasoning has some tiny bit of weight, try substituting any other example of affirming the consequent here. The resulting argument will be just as good. And people do, with some frequency, acquire beliefs on the basis of fallacious reasoning.)

WILLIAMS'S ARGUMENT AGAINST DISTINGUISHING JUSTIFYING AND EXPLAINING REASONS

Let us turn now to Williams's claim that "it must be a mistake simply to separate explanatory and normative reasons." Since, as I said above, Williams seems clearly to accept the ordinary-language distinction for which I have been arguing, he will not, presumably, want to deny anything said so far against Stampe (or at least not want to deny anything because he doesn't accept this distinction). Rather, he argues that if we separate explaining and justifying reasons too sharply, we will no longer be able to make sense of how an agent can act for a reason that is also a justification for his action. "If it is true that a has a reason to ϕ," he says, "then it must be possible that he should ϕ for that reason; and if he does act for that reason, then that reason will be the explanation of his acting."

This seems true enough, but the puzzle is why it should be thought inconsistent with distinguishing explaining reasons from justifying reasons. Suppose that I have a reason (a good reason) to go to campus (a class I am teaching meets today, say). Then, as Williams says, it must be possible that I should go to campus for this reason. And this certainly does seem possible. It might well happen that I go to campus and that my reason for going is that a class I am teaching meets today. Also, he says, "if [I do] act for that reason, then that reason will be the explanation of [my] acting." But again, this seems perfectly unproblematic. The fact that my class meets today is a reason for me to go to campus. And when I do go to campus because my class meets today, then my reason for going (my class meets today) explains my going. So where is the problem? So far as I can see, in telling this exciting little story, nowhere did I use a sense of "reason" other than one of the four distinguished above.

I suspect that Williams would say that there has been an equivocation in my telling this story, one that allows me to shift illegitimately between justifying and explaining senses of "reason" at a crucial point. It is in essence the equivocation I noted in my discussion of (2) above. What gives me a reason to go to campus (and so justifies my going, if I do) is the fact that a class I am teaching meets today. But when I go, it is not the *fact* that a class I am teaching meets today that explains my going, it is my awareness of this fact (or perhaps we should say that it is my belief or judgment that this is a fact). It is my *thinking* that a class I am teaching meets today that explains my going, not the fact that it does. So the equivocation I suspect that Williams would hold to exist in the story above occurs in the shift from saying that it is the fact that a class I am teaching meets today that gives me *a* reason to go to campus to saying that when I do go, *my* reason for going is that this class meets today. Strictly speaking, the claim should be that my reason for going, if it is to explain my going, must be that I think (or judge, believe, etc.) that this class meets today. But once we see this, it will seem that some further element is needed as well. The mere awareness of the fact that a class I am teaching meets today (or belief that it does) seems not by itself enough to move me to go to campus unless in *some* sense I want to meet this class.

This, Williams holds, is a general point, which he puts by saying that any explanation of an agent's actions must make reference to that agent's "actual motivational set," abbreviated as "*S*." "When the reason is an explanation of [the agent's] action," he says, "then of course it will be, in some form, in his *S*, because certainly—and nobody denies this—what he actually does has to be explained by his *S*" (Williams 1989, 5). This is, I take it, the same point that Davidson (1980, 5) makes by saying that an agent's reason for performing an action under some description must consist of the agent's having a pro attitude toward actions with some property and his belief that the action, under this description, has the property.

So it would appear, according to this line of thought, that strict adherence to the distinction between justifying reasons ((3) and (4) above) and explaining reasons ((2) above) forces us into the absurd position of holding that the sort of fact that can give me a reason to act, as the fact that a class I am teaching meets today seems to give me a reason to go to campus, can never be *my* reason for so acting, since my reason is supposed to explain my action and hence must consist not of facts independent of me but of my own subjective states (or propositional attitudes, etc.), which are the only things that can explain actions.

Williams's own solution to this problem, as we have seen, is to adopt the internal-reasons account of justifying reasons, which in essence is the view that (to put it a bit loosely) an agent has a reason to perform some action only if the agent has some motive that could move him or her to perform the action.[8] It is this connection with the agent's motive that is supposed to insure that the same fact that provides a reason for him to perform the action provides an explanation of it when the action is actually performed. This connection thus bridges the apparent gap between justifying and explaining reasons. In doing so, presumably, it shows why, as Williams thinks, it is "a mistake simply to separate" the two.[9]

But, I want to say, this is not a mistake. I want to defend the distinction between justifying reasons and explaining reasons by arguing, first, that if the gap that the internal-reasons view tries to bridge really exists, then, perhaps surprisingly, this view fails to bridge it and, second, that in fact this gap doesn't exist anyway. So if I am right, there is no genuine problem here for the internal-reasons view to solve.

Does the internal-reasons account of justifying reasons actually solve the problem apparently created by sharply distinguishing justifying reasons from explaining reasons, as I did in explaining (2) and (3) above? I think the answer is no, but there is a way of stating the problem, the way in which Williams states it, where it appears to be yes. We can put the problem by saying that if justifying reasons are to move us, if they are to be the reasons on which we act, then they must somehow include our motives (or items in our "actual motivational sets"), since, of course, these are the only things that can possibly move us. This, in a nut shell, is the main, perhaps the only, argument for the internal-reasons account.

But, I want to say, even if we accept the idea that justifying reasons, in order to *be* justifying reasons, must be capable of moving us, the internal-reasons view doesn't show how this happens, because it puts motives "in" reasons in the wrong place. The question to ask here is whether, in the fullest or most accurate specification available to the agent, the description of whatever it is that provides the agent with a reason to ϕ (say to go to campus) must include a reference to something in his or her motivational set. The internal-reasons view is committed to saying that it must. Indeed, one might say, this is the very essence of the internal-reasons account of justifying reasons. According to Williams, "A has a reason to ϕ only if he could reach the conclusion to ϕ by a sound deliberative route *from the motivations he already has*" (1989, 2; emphasis added). In an earlier paper he said, "The internal reasons conception is concerned with the agent's rationality. What we can correctly ascribe to him in a third-personal internal reason statement is also what he can ascribe to himself as a result of deliberation" (Williams 1979, 103).

What this means is that on the internal-reasons view, the *content* of the justifying reason, and so the contents of the judgments or beliefs of the agent who is rationally deliberating, if it is really to be a reason, must always involve, in an essential way, reference to some element of the agent's motivational set, at least when this content is fully explicit. In terms of our example, what gives me a reason to go to campus will have to be not just the fact that a class I am teaching meets today but this fact *plus* the fact that I have (what Williams calls) a motivation of some sort toward meeting this class. (In discussing Williams's argument I will use "desire" to refer to the elements of what he calls the agent's subjective motivational set.)

But unfortunately this doesn't solve the original problem that the internal reasons account was supposed to solve. The original problem was supposed to be that whatever facts give me a justifying reason to do something, these facts, just by themselves, won't explain my acting as I have reason to act until we add some subjective elements, in particular, *both* my awareness of the facts in question *and* the associated desire of mine. This is not changed by the internal-reason theorist claiming that the facts that give me a justifying reason to act always include desires of mine. On the internal-reasons view, what gives me a good reason to go to campus will be the fact that a class I am teaching is meeting today *plus* the fact that I have some sort of motivation toward meeting this class. But what *explains* my going to campus, according to this way of thinking, will not be these *facts* but rather (at least) my judgment or belief that a class I am teaching meets today and I have a desire to meet this class. But then, of course, since, according to this view, *mere* beliefs are not enough to move me, to explain my action we will need yet *another* desire, my desire to meet classes that I believe I have this first sort of desire to meet. If proponents of this view allow that I can be moved by this *belief* all by itself, then no desires are needed to explain actions after all, since such a belief, like any belief, could be false. I might not have the desire I believe I have.

It is very important to distinguish the facts or alleged facts referred to or described in the *content* of my reason judgment from the facts about me that are supposed to explain my action. The fact that a class I am teaching meets today gives me a reason to go to campus (I would say). But my judgment or belief that a class I am teaching meets today (plus, according to the view we are considering, my desire to meet this class) explains my going. The internal-reasons view holds that the mere fact that a class I am teaching meets today is not by itself enough to give me a good reason to go to campus. I must also have a motive of some sort toward meeting this class. That is, according to the internal-reasons view, the *content* of my reason judgment (which, if true, will actually give me a good reason to act) will be not "A class I am teaching meets today" but "A class I am teaching meets today *and* I have a desire of some sort toward meeting this class." Hence the desire needed to explain my going to campus *can't* be the one referred to *in* this judgment. One can act on false reason judgments. So I may fail actually to have a desire to meet this class and yet still act on this judgment (just as I might if the class I am teaching does not actually meet today). And in any case, the desire that *moves* me will have to be one that has as its content the *same* content as my reason judgment, which, on the internal-reasons view, will be that a class I am teaching meets today *and* I have a desire to meet this class. So the motive needed to explain my going to campus will have to be *another* desire, i.e., roughly a desire I have to meet classes of mine that I *believe* I have a desire of some sort to meet.

So the internal-reasons view doesn't solve the original problem after all. The gap between the facts that are supposed to give me justifying reasons for acting and the subjective elements—beliefs and desires roughly—that are needed to explain my acting on these facts, if it was there at all, still remains. It doesn't bridge this gap *at all* simply to include motives (or desires) of mine *among* the facts that give me justifying reasons to act. This merely gives the implausible result that we now need a *further* desire of mine (toward acting on the desire I judge myself to have) to explain my action.[10] But the gap is still there, if it ever was, since just as I might fail to have a desire to meet my class, so I might fail to have a desire to act on the desire to meet my class that I judge myself to have. And just as, on the original view, what gave me a justifying reason for going to campus—the fact that a class I am teaching meets today—wasn't by itself enough to explain my going to campus (since I might fail to be aware of this fact), so, on the internal-reasons view, what gives me a reason to go—the original fact plus my desire to act on it—still isn't enough to explain my going. I might, after all, fail to be aware that a class I am teaching meets today and/or that I have a desire to teach this class. I need to *believe* or judge that the original fact obtains and that I have a desire to act on it, *and* I need to have (not just believe I have) a desire to act on desires of the first sort. So the internal-reasons theory doesn't bridge the supposed gap at all.

The "solution" to the problem of the gap between justifying and explaining reasons, I suggest, is to realize that there is no gap that needs to be bridged. Three ideas combine to produce the thought that there is a gap that needs to be bridged between these two senses of "reason," i.e., that it would be a mistake to sharply distinguish them. First, as Williams puts it, "If it is true that A has a reason to ϕ, then it must be possible that he should ϕ for that reason; and if he does act for that reason, then that reason will be the explanation of his acting" (1989, 5). Second, it is thought that whatever fact it is that gives me reason to ϕ can't be, by itself, what explains my ϕ-ing when I do, since my judgment that this fact obtains is also needed to explain my acting. And then, third, since supposedly beliefs or judgments alone cannot move us to act, a desire of some sort is also required.

But the first two points by themselves are innocuous, they produce no gap, while the third point produces a gap only if we understand it to say something false. When some fact p gives me a reason to ϕ and then I ϕ "for that reason," this surely only means that I ϕ-ed because I believed or judged that p. And *in this sense* "that reason will be the explanation of [my] acting." That is, when I ϕ-ed because I believed or judged that p, the *fact* that p will explain my ϕ-ing, and hence "my reason for ϕ-ing was that p." It is true that we say both "Ralph's reason for leaving early was that he had another appointment" and "Ralph's reason for leaving early was that he believed he had another appointment." But this is only because we sometimes don't want to commit ourselves to the truth of the proposition that allegedly describes the agent's reason here. Sentences of the form "s's reason for a-ing was that p" (that is, (2) above) commit anyone who asserts them to holding that p. It would just be a mistake to move from the idea that an agent must be aware of some fact, or believe that it is a fact, in order to be moved to action by it, to the conclusion that somehow this fact cannot by itself give him reason to act. This would be like holding that since I must be *aware* that there are three bottles of beer in the refrigerator and that there are three more on the table to conclude that there are six bottles altogether, these facts by themselves aren't enough to give me reason to conclude that there are six bottles altogether.

So there is nothing in either of the first two points that is inconsistent with a sharp distinction between explaining and justifying reasons. It is the third idea, that some *further* desire or motivating state is always part of the agent's reason for acting, that seems to create a gap between justifying and explaining reasons, since now there seems to be something required for explaining reasons that is not present in justifying reasons, namely desires (or in Williams's terms, elements in the agent's motivational set). Hence the internalist attempt to bridge this gap by putting desires too into justifying reasons. But, as we have already seen above, if it is to avoid obvious counterexamples, the idea that desires are always needed to move us to act is plausible only if we understand "desire" in the broadest possible sense, the sense for which I use the term "pro attitude." And in this sense, *whatever* moves me to go to campus will count as a pro attitude of mine toward going to campus, *including* my belief that a class I am teaching is meeting today. So the only sense in which the third idea above is true is one in which no element beyond my belief or judgment that p is required for inclusion in my reason for ϕ-ing.

I conclude that neither Stampe's ordinary-language considerations nor Williams's argument from practical reason has provided any sound reason to reject a sharp distinction between explaining and justifying reasons. If this is right, then at least one of what Williams calls the "fundamental motivations" for the internal-reasons account of justifying reasons is not sound (see Williams 1989, 5). Nor, of course, is the defense of this account against the charge that, in its only plausible form, it is not distinguishable from externalism, which depends on breaking down the distinction between explaining and justifying reasons.

In this chapter we have been looking at a view, the internal-reasons account of justifying reasons, that holds it to be a necessary condition of having a justifying reason for acting that the agent have a desire of some sort. I want to shift now to a view that holds that having a desire (that is, a desire proper) of a particular sort is a sufficient condition for having a justifying reason for acting to satisfy the desire. This is the view that we have already encountered briefly at the end of chapter 1 in connection with Platts's attempt to give a philosophical taxonomy of desires, namely Stephen Schiffer's claim that some desires are what he calls "reason providing."

Desires as Justifying Reasons:

Part 2, Reason-Providing Desires and

the Practical Syllogism

Once we see the crucial distinction between pro attitudes and desires proper, the idea contained in the internal-reasons theory—that having a desire of some sort is a necessary condition for having a justifying reason to perform an action—will only seem plausible if we are using the pro-attitude sense of "desire." But as we have seen, such a necessary condition on justifying reasons is one that any externalist should be happy to accept. So in essence, I am arguing that one can think that the internal-reasons account of justifying reasons is a contentious or skeptical account that rules out some important class of things that philosophers have held to be good reasons for acting, such as considerations of justice or duty or the like, only if one mistakenly thinks that the term "desire" (or "motive," etc.), as it is used in this theory, must be taken as referring to desires proper rather than to pro attitudes.

An intuitively much less contentious claim is that at least some proper desires are, all by themselves, enough to give the person who has them good reason to act to satisfy them, i.e., that having some desire proper is a sufficient condition for having a justifying reason to satisfy that desire. On its face, it is not quite so plausible to make this claim for all desires proper. Whims, for instance, aren't always thought to provide good reasons to act on them, even by those who have them. On the other hand, some desires, such as a craving for some harmless food for which one has a taste, do seem to provide one with reason to act on them (other things being equal, at least). If I have a craving for the taste of sweet and sour pork, for instance, it would seem that this craving all by itself makes satisfying it attractive to me, that is, gives me a reason to have some sweet and sour pork, or anyway to have something with this taste. If I did not have this craving, then it would seem that, other things being equal, I would not have a reason (or this reason) to have something with this taste. Yet if I have the craving, I also have a reason to satisfy it. Desires of this sort, then, would seem to be among the best possible examples of desires that give the person who has them good reason to act to satisfy them. An account of this has been proposed by Stephen Schiffer (1976), who has developed the thought that there are at least some proper desires of this sort, that is, desires that automatically provide the person who has them with good reason to act to satisfy them. So it will be worth looking closely at Schiffer's account of these desires.

SCHIFFER'S "REASON-PROVIDING DESIRES"

Schiffer in essence accepts Nagel's distinction between motivated and unmotivated desires (though he calls the former "reason-following desires"). He argues, however, that what he calls "reason-providing desires" (or "r-p desires" for short) make up a proper subset of unmotivated desires (and hence they will make up a proper subset of what I have labeled desires proper). These are explained by Schiffer as follows:

When it is an r-p-desire to ϕ that one acts on, the reason for which one ϕ's and, typically, the only reason one has to ϕ, is provided entirely by one's desire to ϕ and . . . one's reason for ϕ-ing is just that desire; this, of course, is one reason I call such desires "reason-providing." At this moment I have not the least desire to eat an ice cream or . . . to scratch my nose; but if I now had an r-p-desire to do either of those things I would have a good and sufficient reason for doing it.

. . . R-p-desires . . . provide the reasons, the justifications, for themselves. There is never a reason for which one has an r-p-desire, one never has an r-p-desire because one thinks of what one desires as being desirable in a certain way; one does, however, find desirable what one has an r-p-desire for, and because what is desired is desirable in the way found desirable, one does have reason to desire what one desires, and one's desire is, in the absence of defeating considerations, justified. It is, therefore, not because a thing is desirable in a certain way that one has an r-p-desire for it; quite the contrary, it is desirable in that way precisely because one has the desire, and it is thus that r-p-desires provide reasons for themselves, thus that they are self-justifying.

And yet, this also is true: when one acts on an r-p-desire—one acts for the gain of pleasure and the relief of discomfort—usually both, always one or the other—that one's action affords; it is for that that one acts and that is why one acts, and because one's action is made desirable by its connection with pleasure and discomfort, one's desire is justified.

. . . An r-p-desire is a self-referential desire for its own gratification; an r-p-desire to ϕ is a desire to ϕ to relieve the discomfort of that desire, a desire to ϕ for the pleasure of its own relief. So a thirst is a desire to drink, a discomforting desire to drink, a discomforting desire to drink which would be pleasurable to relieve, a desire to drink to gratify itself. (Schiffer 1976, 198–199)

Thus what Schiffer calls r-p desires are supposed to have at least the following features:

1. They provide "good and sufficient" reason for performing the actions for which they are desires (in the absence of defeating or contrary considerations, presumably).

2. They are self-justifying, i.e., they provide the reasons,

the justifications, for themselves in the absence of defeating considerations.

3. They aim at the gain of pleasure or relief of discomfort, or both, that the action affords.

4. They are self-referential (in a way in which other un-motivated desires are not, presumably).

Beside the examples he gives in the passages quoted, Schiffer uses as his main example of an r-p desire a craving to eat chocolate, and he mentions that this might take the form of a craving throughout dinner to eat chocolate mousse for dessert. He also says, "The aroused bodily appetites are of course the examples *par excellence* of r-p-desires" (Schiffer 1976, 202).

Since we wish to consider the first and most con-tentious of these features, being "reason-providing," it makes sense to ask whether having some or all of the other three features listed will be enough to show that what are being *called* "reason-providing desires" really are reason-providing in the way Schiffer thinks. This is the main question that I will pursue here. But there is a logically prior question that we will need to look at as well. This is the question of whether what Schiffer calls "r-p desires" are really "one thing" (as Socrates might have put it). That is, there is a question of whether the features Schiffer as-signs to r-p desires succeed in coherently describing a kind of desire that exists, that people have, and that differs importantly from other kinds of desires they have. If this is not the case, then the question of whether these desires are actually entitled to be called "reason-providing" will be moot.

So let us consider, to begin with, the argument Schiffer gives for the second of the four features delineated, i.e., the claim that r-p desires are self-justifying. All the steps of his explicit argument for this claim are given in the second of the paragraphs quoted above. They are these: First, r-p desires are not desires that one has for a reason, which is to say, I take it, that they are unmotivated desires. Second, "one does, however, find desirable what one has an r-p-desire for." Hence, third, "because what is desired is desirable in the way found desirable, one does have reason to desire what one desires," that is, one's desire is justified, at least in the absence of defeating considerations.

This argument, however, is not valid as it stands. There is a logical gap between step 2, which says that the person who has an r-p desire *finds* the object of this desire desirable, and step 3, which says that the object of this desire *is* desirable in the way found desirable. Schiffer is right in emphasizing the difference between saying that someone desires something because he or she finds it desirable (which would make the desire a motivated desire) and saying that the agent finds it desirable because he or she desires it (which presumably makes it what Schiffer calls an r-p desire). But this by itself doesn't yield the conclusion Schiffer wants here, because in general there is a difference between my finding something desirable and its being desirable. To say that I "find something desirable" might mean just that I do desire it, of course, but that clearly doesn't do Schiffer's argument any good. It might also mean that I regard the thing as being desirable, i.e., roughly that I think it has some value, is worth desiring. This, however, is something about which I can be mistaken. So we can't argue simply from the fact that I think something is desirable, that it seems desirable to me, to the conclusion that it really is desirable.

There is a fairly obvious reply Schiffer could make here. This would be to argue that the point we are considering, that r-p desires are self-justifying, is not intended to be independent of the first point, that r-p desires are actually reason-providing. Rather, the reply goes, that r-p

84 desires are self-justifying follows from the claim that they are actually reason-providing. Schiffer doesn't explicitly say this, but he may want to hold this view, and in any case, it seems true. If my craving to eat chocolate all by itself gives me a good reason to eat chocolate and we accept the plausible principle that some action of mine is desirable if I have good reason to do it, then my desire to eat chocolate will indeed be self-justifying in just the way Schiffer says. In this case, what I find desirable (that is, what I have an r-p desire for) will be desirable just because I have this desire. My unmotivated r-p desire to eat chocolate will provide me with a reason to eat chocolate (i.e., will make my eating chocolate desirable) and will thus "automatically" be a desire to do something I have good reason to do, something that it is desirable that I do.

This is a very plausible claim to make here and, as I said, may be what Schiffer himself intends. The only drawback is that taking this line means that the really contentious claim, that r-p desires actually provide justifying reasons for acting, is simply assumed. So we can't appeal, without circularity, to the claim that r-p desires are self-justifying to support the assertion that they are actually reason-providing. In fact, I think the connection between these two points is closer than I have so far made it seem or than it appears at first sight. This is because on a natural reading of "self-justifying" it will be true not only that the claim that r-p desires are reason-providing entails the claim that they are self-justifying but also that the second entails the first, that is, that these two claims are logically equivalent.

If we understand the claim that a desire is justified to mean that, as Schiffer puts it, one has "reason to desire what one desires," then a desire will be *self*-justifying when the desire by itself provides one with a reason to desire what it is a desire for. But a desire that by itself provides

DESIRES AS JUSTIFYING REASONS

one with a reason to desire what it is a desire for is a reason-providing desire. So, as far as I can tell, the first two features in the list above of features that Schiffer claims for r-p desires—that they are reason-providing and that they are self-justifying—are logically equivalent. Any desires that have one of these features will then certainly have the other. Given this, for simplicity I will continue to refer to desires that have both these features as reason-providing desires. The question is whether those desires that Schiffer *calls* "r-p desires" (assuming for the moment that there are such things) have these two logically equivalent features.

The original explanation of r-p desires, given in the first paragraph of the long quotation above, might seem to provide an argument for answering this question affirmatively, but in fact it does not. In that paragraph Schiffer moves from the claim that there are cases of desire where one's reason for acting, and indeed one's only reason for acting, is that one has this desire, to labeling such desires as "reason-providing." But if we understand this to be an argument that such desires really do provide reasons for acting (which it seems to be, since he says, "This . . . is one reason I call such desires 'reason-providing' "), it simply conflates an agent's reasons with justifying reasons. As I hope is clear from my discussion in the last chapter, the fact that some desire of mine is *my* reason for doing something, even my only reason, doesn't entail that it is a good reason.

So if the assertion that what Schiffer calls r-p desires really are reason-providing is to be supported by what Schiffer says, it will have to be by one or both of the other two points he makes about such desires. These involve, respectively, appealing to the connection of r-p desires to pleasure and discomfort (the third of the four features of r-p desires listed above) and appealing to their self-referential feature. Similarly, since the alleged self-justifying nature of r-p desires turns out to be logically equivalent to the claim that they are reason-providing, the question of whether there really is an important kind of desire here at all will reduce to the question of whether what Schiffer says about their connection to pleasure and discomfort, combined with what he says about their self-reference, coherently describes a significant kind of desire.

So let's look at the connection to pleasure and discomfort. In the quotation above, Schiffer says that when one acts on an r-p desire, it is "because one's action is made desirable by its connection with pleasure and discomfort [that] one's desire is justified." This certainly *seems* to say that an r-p desire is justified because it leads to an action made desirable by the fact that it gives pleasure or relieves discomfort. This would be plausible enough (if we accept here the principle that an action is desirable if it brings pleasure or relieves discomfort) except that on its face it doesn't seem compatible with the idea that r-p desires are *themselves* reason-providing. After all, if I perform some action to bring myself some pleasure or to relieve some discomfort, then, in general at least, it is the prospect of this pleasure or relief of discomfort that provides me with reason to act, not my desire to perform an action that I think will have either of these two features. In fact, my desire in such a case would seem to be a motivated desire (or reason-following desire in Schiffer's terms), not an unmotivated desire at all. So it is hard to see how the connection with pleasure and discomfort can be enlisted in aid of the claim that r-p desires are actually reason-providing at all.

Schiffer's answer to this, as I understand it, is to appeal to the fourth characteristic on the list above, self-reference, and to claim that this is essentially connected to the third characteristic, the gain of pleasure and relief of discomfort involved. "An r-p-desire," he says in the passage quoted above, "is a self-referential desire for its own gratification; an r-p-desire to ϕ is a desire to ϕ to relieve the discomfort of that desire, a desire to ϕ for the pleasure of its own relief." So these two characteristics of r-p desires, their connection to pleasure and discomfort and their self-reference, are not distinct. An r-p desire will be essentially an uncomfortable state that *is* a desire for its own relief. "One's desire to ϕ, one's desire to gain the pleasure of satisfying one's desire to ϕ, one's desire to relieve the discomfort of one's desire to ϕ—these are all one and the same desire" (Schiffer 1976, 199). So r-p desires, on this way of understanding them, would seem to be states that have a certain uncomfortable phenomenological character and are themselves desires for the pleasurable relief of that very discomfort.

While this is getting close to what we want, in fact, however, I think that it still isn't quite the best way to understand r-p desires. It at best describes only the clearest or most dramatic cases of r-p desires. Nor, I think, is it really quite what Schiffer intends this term to mean, even though some of the things he says make it sound this way. For one thing, some of his examples of r-p desires pretty obviously don't fit this description. It doesn't seem plausible, for instance, to hold that a craving throughout dinner to have chocolate mousse for dessert need actually be uncomfortable, yet that is one of Schiffer's examples of an r-p desire.

He also says, in a passage already quoted, that "a thirst" would be an r-p desire. But thirst need not be uncomfortable, though Schiffer seems to say that it does. According to him, "a thirst is a desire to drink, a discomforting desire to drink, a discomforting desire to drink which would be pleasurable to relieve" (1976, 199). But this is just not phenomenologically accurate. For most people, the mild thirst they experience at least a few times every day, of the sort that leads them to the water cooler or soft drink machine, has practically no phenomenological character at all, certainly nothing that could be called "discomfort." Schiffer may be thinking of intense thirst. But even if we ignore the fact that most people rarely or never experience intense thirst, it would seem implausible to claim that while intense thirst is a reason-providing desire, everyday thirst is not. Some of his other examples of r-p desires, like a craving for chocolate and such bodily appetites as hunger, do have distinctive phenomenological characters, of course, but at least at the level of intensity that most readers of these words are likely to have experienced most of them, they are no more discomforting than everyday thirst is. In fact, some of these desires, some mild cravings for instance, are rather pleasant.

Then too, some of the things Schiffer himself says about r-p desires don't really fit this description of them as discomforting desires for their own relief, since he implies in several places that one could have an r-p desire that was not itself uncomfortable. For example, he says, "When one acts on an r-p-desire one acts for the gain of pleasure and the relief of discomfort—usually both, always one or the other—that one's action affords" (1976, 198).

So it may well be that Schiffer wants to hold that an r-p desire does not actually need to be uncomfortable, in spite of the way he sometimes speaks. That fits his examples better and doesn't leave us with the implausible consequence that only intense bodily appetites, for instance, are reason-providing, while their everyday versions are not. A puzzle presented by this way of understanding what he says, however, is that if we drop the claim that such r-p desires are themselves uncomfortable, it becomes difficult to understand the self-reference they are supposed to involve in a way that distinguishes them from motivated desires that have the same object, i.e., when these are motivated by the thought that their satisfaction will be pleasurable. Consider, as a contrast to Schiffer's example of someone who (let us say intensely) *craves* chocolate mousse for dessert, a person who (merely) wants to have chocolate mousse for dessert throughout dinner because he or she thinks it would be pleasurable to do so. This is a motivated desire, since the agent has a reason for having it. It need have no particular phenomenological character at all. But it is still a "desire for its own satisfaction" in one straightforward sense, the same sense in which this is true of any desire.

So the idea that there are what Schiffer calls r-p desires faces a dilemma here. It seems clear that we need to connect these desires with the gain of pleasure and the relief of discomfort to make them reason-providing. But this raises the problem of distinguishing these desires, which are supposed to be unmotivated *providers* of reasons, from motivated desires for pleasure and relief of discomfort, which are, in Schiffer's terms, reason-following, not reason-providing. The solution to this problem, which Schiffer at least appears part of the time to offer, is to hold that for these r-p desires, the desire itself is an uncomfortable state to be in and the pleasurable relief of this very discomfort is what one seeks. This is, I think, a coherent description of some genuine desires, but it has the drawback that there are very few actual examples of such desires. It also gives, as I said, the implausible result that while intense thirst, intense hunger, or an intense craving for chocolate are reason-providing, everyday examples of thirst, hunger, and so on, are not, since they are not uncomfortable.

The solution, I suggest—and this may in fact be implicit in some of the things Schiffer himself says—is to relax the requirement that r-p desires be themselves uncomfortable by saying that it is enough that they have a phenomenological character of a sort that makes their satisfaction *automatically* pleasurable (which, I take it, relief of discomfort is). This will be enough to insure that the self-reference of r-p desires is different from that of other sorts of desire. At the same time it won't restrict r-p desires to uncomfortable states such as intense hunger. In general, it is not true that the satisfaction of a desire is automatically pleasurable. I might want chocolate mousse for dessert, get it, and yet not enjoy it at all. And this can happen even if I only wanted it because I thought I would enjoy it. But, the claim will have to be, if my desire for chocolate mousse is an r-p desire, a genuine craving say, then this is not possible. A genuine craving, conceived of in this way, will be an r-p desire because it will be, among other things, a phenomenological state that it is automatically pleasurable to satisfy or fulfill, in the same way in which it is automatically pleasurable to relieve one's own discomfort. So on this account, intense thirst, say, will indeed be an r-p desire and will be, as Schiffer says, "a discomforting desire to drink which would be pleasurable to relieve." But discomfort will not be an essential feature of r-p desires. The essential feature, of which discomfort is just one especially obvious case, will be that the r-p desire is or essentially involves a phenomenological character such that it would automatically be pleasurable to satisfy this desire.

It is not clear that there is a single term for this phenomenological character, that is, one that corresponds to discomfort in the special case of intense hunger or thirst. This may explain why Schiffer simply uses the term "discomfort." Perhaps "craving" is close enough. It seems clear, though, that there are such desires. Schiffer's own examples are perfectly good ones. So we can answer yes to what I called above the "prior question" of whether Schiffer's description of r-p desires coherently describes a kind of desire that people really have. But this still leaves us with the central question about these desires, namely whether what Schiffer calls r-p desires (as we now understand them) are *actually* reason-providing.

The only argument that Schiffer gives for the claim that
they are is the brief and clearly unsatisfactory one already
considered. And we have already seen that the main independent argument he gives for the logically equivalent
claim that r-p desires are self-justifying is not valid without
the addition of the assumption at issue, that r-p desires are
reason-providing. That leaves only the connection with
pleasure and discomfort. Speaking of when one acts on an
r-p desire, Schiffer says that "because one's action is made
desirable by its connection with pleasure and discomfort,
one's desire is justified" (1976, 198). He is clearly assuming here, as I have been through this whole discussion of
r-p desires, that an action is "made desirable" by the fact
that it brings pleasure or relieves discomfort. And in this
context I think we are safe in assuming that actions are
desirable just to the extent that there are good reasons to
perform them. (That is, "desirable" here is not intended to
mean "morally desirable," only "justified" or "rationally
justified.")

I have no quarrel with the claim that there is good
reason for one to perform actions that bring one pleasure
or relieve one's discomfort. But if this principle really is
essential to the reason-providing property of r-p desires,
then it is not the fact that they are *desires* for certain things
that connects r-p desires to justifying reasons but rather the
fact that they have the phenomenological character of being automatically pleasurable to satisfy.

Compare such an r-p desire with another unmotivated
desire with the same or an analogous content, a whim that
just strikes me one afternoon, say. To make the comparison
work, this whim can't have any of the phenomenological

character of an r-p desire (roughly, craving), nor can it be motivated by anything, such as the thought that I would like or enjoy whatever is its object. Perhaps Anscombe's famous case of a desire to drink a saucer of mud would be an example here, as long as we don't think of this as a craving of any sort. So compare this with an r-p desire, a craving, say, with the same content, i.e., it is a desire to drink a saucer of mud. The only difference between these two cases will be that the r-p desire has a phenomenological character such that satisfying it is automatically pleasurable. This can be true even if drinking the saucer of mud is not, and is not expected by the agent to be, an *inherently* pleasurable experience. (As Schiffer puts it, "because the anticipated pleasure is itself the pleasure of satisfying that [r-p] desire, nothing remains to preclude the frustrating but not unheard of experience of an intense desire for chocolate, or whatever, the satisfaction of which brings and was expected to bring only a little pleasure" [1976, 202].) In fact, the whole argument for saying that r-p desires are reason-providing depends on the agent's *not* thinking of the object of such desires as inherently pleasurable. His or her doing so would turn it into a motivated desire.

We have already seen that we need to distinguish two very different questions. There is a difference between asking what gives an agent a reason to do something (i.e., what, if anything, justifies his or her doing it), and what moves an agent to do something (what explains his or her doing it). If we keep firmly in mind the comparison between an r-p desire to drink a saucer of mud and a mere whim with the same content but with no phenomenological character at all (or at least without the special phenomenological character of r-p desires), it is clear enough that when the agent acts on either of these desires, the answer to the explanatory question is the same. The *agent's* reason for drinking the mud will be that he or she had that desire (the whim or the r-p desire) to do so. So even when one acts on a whim of this sort, which though not an r-p desire is still an unmotivated desire, it will still be true that "the reason for which one ϕ's . . . is provided entirely by one's desire to ϕ and . . . one's reason for ϕ-ing is just that desire," just as it is for an r-p desire.

The difference is that with the r-p desire, but perhaps not the whim, it is also true that there is a reason, that is, a good reason, to drink the saucer of mud. In the case of the r-p desire, but not the whim, doing so is certain to be pleasurable because of the special phenomenological character of r-p desires. What this shows is that r-p desires provide justifying reasons for acting on them not in virtue of being desires but in virtue of having the special phenomenological character they have. Schiffer (1976, 199) seems to hold that this phenomenological character is not separable from the desire itself (from which it follows, as he notes, that on his view desires are not to be identified solely in terms of their content, since then, in our example, the r-p desire and the whim would be the same desire). But that is not so obvious.

It seems quite clear, for instance, that one can feel hungry, that is, one can have feelings with the same phenomenological character as hunger, while (at least) not being at all in need of food. Can one have such feelings without wanting to eat? It is hard to see why not. If one knew perfectly well that one did not need food, for instance, one might come to interpret such feelings, i.e., with the same phenomenological character as those usually associated with need for food, as something else. (I sometimes have what certainly seem to me to be exactly the same feelings that I have when hungry shortly *after* a very large meal, for instance, and have come to understand them, in *this* context, as feeling stuffed with food.) Internal bodily sensations, such as those associated with hunger, surely stand in need of interpretation even if, as also seems true, we have all learned to interpret them correctly very early in life. But just *as sensations,* that is, as having a specific phenomenological character, they are, so to speak, uninterpreted. Why can't this be the case even when the phenomenological character in question is such that the (typically) associated desire would be automatically pleasurable to satisfy?

What emerges from this, I think, is that an r-p desire, in our example of a craving to drink a saucer of mud, can be understood as involving several logically distinct features: (1) the agent has one of several possible bodily sensations, (2) the agent correctly understands or interprets the sensation as making drinking a saucer of mud pleasurable (as might be the case, for instance, if there is some underlying physiological state, analogous to an empty stomach in the case of hunger, that gives rise to this sensation and will terminate by giving the agent a pleasurable sensation when he or she has consumed a saucer of mud), and (3) the agent has a desire to drink a saucer of mud. It is probably true that we do not correctly *describe* a person as having a craving to drink a saucer of mud unless all three features were present. But it doesn't follow from this that the three features are not distinct, which, as I said, seems to be Schiffer's view. After all, one could have a bodily sensation that one correctly interpreted as making drinking a saucer of mud pleasurable while thinking (even mistakenly, perhaps) that this sort of pleasure gave one no reason to pursue it, and so while having no desire to drink a saucer of mud.

If this is right and what Schiffer calls r-p desires are, so to speak, complexes of these three elements, then it is easy to see that they are not, after all, reason-providing, any more than are other unmotivated desires, such as whims. Suppose that I have the first two items in the list above without the third. That is, suppose that I have some bodily sensation or sensations that I correctly interpret as making drinking a saucer of mud pleasurable to me. Then, other things being equal, whether or not I have a good reason to drink a saucer of mud will depend on whether or not I have good reason to do what will be pleasurable to me. The addition of the third element, a desire to drink a saucer of mud, changes nothing one way or the other.

In fact, so far as I can tell, though this last point is easier to see if we imagine the desire involved in an r-p desire as an element separate from the bodily sensation with a special phenomenological character, nothing really changes if we deny that these are distinct elements and simply say, as Schiffer wants to, that it is the desire itself that has this phenomenological character. Since I want to hold the principle that, other things being equal, I have good reason to do what will be pleasurable to me, I also want to hold that what Schiffer calls r-p desires are reason-providing, in the sense that whenever I have one of these desires (however we analyze it), satisfying the desire will automatically be pleasurable to me. But the question of whether or not there really is a justifying reason in such a situation depends completely on the truth of this principle. Someone who denies this principle can, with total consistency, agree that there are what Schiffer calls r-p desires but deny that they are reason-providing.

So r-p desires appear as a kind of hybrid, if we recall the earlier discussion of motivated and unmotivated desires in chapter 1. Motivated desires were there defined as ones the agent has for a reason, as when I want to see my sister and her family next summer because I know her children are growing up and that next summer will be one of my few chances to see them. On this definition, r-p desires will be unmotivated. At the same time both Nagel and Schiffer apparently hold that while what (if anything) justifies an action performed on the basis of a motivated desire is whatever reasons the agent has for holding that desire, an action performed on the basis of an unmotivated desire will be justified, if it is, only if the desire itself provides the agent with a good reason to satisfy it. But in the case of r-p desires, this is not obviously so. Though r-p desires are unmotivated, I will be justified in acting on an r-p desire (i.e., I will have good reason to act so as to satisfy it) only if I have good reason to do what brings me pleasure. That is, when I act on r-p desires, it is not obviously the case that my action is justified only if my reason for so acting is a good reason. My reason for eating some chocolate might be that I had a craving for chocolate. But my eating the chocolate was justified, if it was, only if I had good reason to do what I find pleasurable. So this will be a counterexample to the principle that my action is justified only if my reason for acting is a good reason, unless Schiffer is right in thinking that the "automatic" pleasure-producing feature of an r-p desire is somehow identical with, or an essential feature of, this desire. Otherwise, an action done because one has a craving or some other such r-p desire will be justified (to the extent to which it is) because it is pleasurable, but one's reason for performing it will be to satisfy one's desire for chocolate (or whatever), not to get pleasure.

This principle—that an action is rationally justified only if the agent's reason for performing it was a good reason—is, so to speak, the mirror image of the principle that Williams cited in arguing that it is a mistake to sharply distinguish explaining and justifying reasons. ("If it is true that A has a reason to ϕ," Williams claimed, "then it must be possible that he should ϕ for that reason; and if he does act for that reason, then that reason will be the explanation of his acting.") Williams was arguing that it must be possible for good reasons to be explanatory. We saw that this principle is correct and supports his "internal reasons" theory only if we understand the theory as employing the pro-attitude sense of "desire." What this discussion of r-p desires suggests is that the mirror image of Williams's principle, which says that when an action is rationally justified, the explanatory reasons for performing it must be justifying reasons (i.e., that an action is rationally justified only if the agent's reason for performing it was a good reason) is not true at all.

It is not plausible, as I said, to hold that all unmotivated desires provide one with good reasons to act to satisfy them, since this doesn't seem true of mere whims, for instance. A desire that has nothing more to be said in its favor than that I have it might seem more like a pathological state, if only a very mild one, than a good reason for satisfying it. (At the same time, it is not obviously *un*reasonable to act on a whim if nothing [or nothing much] argues against doing so. These features of whims can be understood, I think, in terms of the suggestion made at the end of this chapter.) That is why Schiffer's attempt to distinguish a specific class of unmotivated desires as "reason-providing" seems important. Surprisingly, though, there seems to be nothing about these desires as desires that makes them reason-providing. It is only because the phenomenological character of a desire makes satisfying the desire automatically pleasurable that the desire is reason-providing, via the principle that one has reason to do what will bring one pleasure.

THE PRACTICAL SYLLOGISM

In both this chapter and the last we have been looking at arguments purporting to show that desires of some sort play an essential role in the justification of actions, because they provide either necessary or sufficient conditions for an agent having good reasons for acting as he or she does. The results, so far at least, have been all negative. Neither Williams's internal-reasons view nor Schiffer's account of r-p desires establishes the sort of connection between good reasons and desires proper that it purports to establish. This might seem surprising if one thinks that desires of one sort or another must somehow be involved in the justification of actions. So before I turn, in the next chapter, to the issue of how desires, both pro attitudes and desires proper, figure in the explanation of action, it will be useful to step back from the sort of detailed arguments considered so far, arguments for a connection between desires and justifying reasons, and instead look briefly at a doctrine that seems both widely accepted and widely regarded as showing that some sort of desire must always figure into the justification of action.

Many philosophers, following Aristotle, have held that practical reasoning is best understood in terms of what is usually called the practical syllogism. It may well be that acceptance of this idea by philosophers is what lies behind the thought that there must be some necessary connection between desires and justifying reasons. At the very least, acceptance of the practical syllogism as a paradigm of practical rationality typically embodies the thought that there is such a necessary connection. But (I want to say) it would be extremely surprising if, unlike virtually all other sorts of reasoning, practical reasoning always had (or, to be valid, always should have) a syllogistic form. And in fact I will argue that the idea that it should have such a form is simply false. But this means that I will need to explain how such a (to my mind, deeply implausible) doctrine could continue to be rather widely held.

A contemporary advocate of the practical syllogism, Robert Audi, suggests,

The simplest basic schema for practical reasoning—a schema of which there are numerous variants—consists of a motivational premise; a cognitive, means-end premise; and, as conclusion, a practical judgment. We might represent this schema as follows:

Major Premise—the motivational premise: I want ϕ;

Minor Premise—the cognitive premise: My A-ing would contribute to realizing ϕ;

Conclusion—the practical judgment: I should A.

(Audi 1989, 99)

Most contemporary advocates of the practical syllogism describe it in much this way. Colin McGinn, for instance, after describing the practical syllogism in virtually the same terms, says, "Whenever an agent acts for a reason we can assume some such reasoning to have occurred. We can thus say that an action is a bodily movement issuing from such practical reasoning as is codified in the practical syllogism" (1979, 24). Other philosophers who hold this same general view have said that the conclusion of the practical syllogism is not a judgment but an action. G. E. M. Anscombe, for instance, writes, "There are indeed three types of case. There is the theoretical syllogism, and also the idle practical syllogism which is just a classroom example. In both of these the conclusion is 'said' by the mind which infers it. And there is the practical syllogism proper. Here the conclusion is an action whose point is shewn by the premises, which are now, so to speak, on active service" (1963, 60). So Anscombe would presumably hold that the Audi's "basic schema for practical reasoning" only applies to what she calls "idle" reasoning and that the conclusion of practical reasoning proper is not the judgment that I should A but just my actual act of A-ing. I'll return below to Anscombe's claim that the conclusion of practical reasoning is an action.[1] At this point, however,

I will focus on Audi's description of the practical syllogism given above. (How damaging to Audi's actual position the arguments below against the practical syllogism are depends, of course, on how exactly he means us to understand his claim that this is only "the simplest basic schema," one "of which there are numerous variants.")

A powerful, indeed decisive, reason for thinking that the practical syllogism could not possibly be the basic form that practical reasoning either does or should take has been given by Donald Davidson in the context of discussing weakness of will. The case Davidson considers is one where an agent has conflicting motives or reasons, e.g., where the agent thinks the same act would be both pleasurable and morally objectionable. In such a situation, Davidson says, "We must observe that *this* [practical-syllogism] *picture of moral reasoning is not merely inadequate to account for incontinence; it cannot give a correct account of simple cases of moral conflict.* By a case of moral conflict I mean a case where there are good reasons both for performing an action and for performing one that rules it out (perhaps refraining from the action)" (1970, 33). Davidson's use of "moral" here may be a bit misleading. The problem he is pointing to affects all practical reasoning. The problem is that we frequently find ourselves with what we ourselves regard as good reasons both for and against performing some action we are considering. Practical reasoning often involves weighing up such conflicting considerations in order to decide which to act on. But the practical syllogism gives no hint as to how this weighing up should be done. It has room for only one motive, that is, for only one "consideration," that the agent doing the reasoning thinks argues in favor of some action.

This is, as I said, a decisive argument against the idea that the practical syllogism somehow gives the basic form of practical reasoning. What is it, then, that leads some philosophers to hold that, as Audi puts it, the basic schema for practical reasoning is syllogistic in form? This is what I will try to explain.

When someone is engaged in what is sometimes called theoretical reasoning, it is important to carefully distinguish the assertions or judgments that the reasoner makes (utters or writes down or rehearses in his or her mind) from the propositional content of those judgments. If my belief that p and my belief that if p then q are what have led me to believe that q, then an important part of the justification of my belief that q will be the fact that q is entailed by the propositional content of the beliefs that led me to believe that q. The sentences or propositions that constitute the content of the beliefs that lead me to draw my conclusion that q have certain logical (or perhaps other) relations among themselves, whether or not I believe them. And these relations are important, in fact essential, in deciding whether my reasoning actually supports the belief or judgment that I base on it. (This is not to deny that there are other considerations that are also important, such as whether the beliefs that led me to believe that q are themselves justified.)

Discussions of practical reasoning, of course, need to take account of exactly the same distinction. As Audi puts it,

It is essential that we distinguish between a practical argument as a structure of propositions (or other bearers of truth value, such as perhaps equivalence classes of sentences) and the process of passing, in the way we do in reasoning, from the premises of such a structure to its conclusion. . . . Similarly, we must distinguish between the conclusion of a practical argument, which I take to be a proposition, and what corresponds to it in [someone's] reasoning: his *concluding* that reasoning, by inferring the conclusion from the premises. Typically, the conclusion will be [a] kind of proposition . . . , and the concluding of the reasoning . . . will be an instance of *judging* that the action in question is, say, necessary for realizing the end in view. (1989, 90)

Here, then, is the puzzle. If, like Audi, we distinguish, on the one side, the propositional content and the corresponding argument or "structure of propositions" involved in some piece of practical reasoning from, on the other side, the bearers of this content, that is, the beliefs or judgments (or other mental states, properties, entities, or events) of the agent doing the reasoning, then what reason is there to suppose that the propositions thus distinguished are or (in order to be valid) should be arranged in the syllogistic structure Audi and Anscombe discuss? Likewise, what reason is there to hold that there is or must be a particular "motivational premise" giving what the agent wants, or a "cognitive premise" stating how to get it?

These are not claims that can get any support at all from "the structure of practical reasoning," if we take this to mean looking at how people *actually* reason about how to act. What beliefs or judgments actually lead some agent at some time to judge that he or she should perform some action, and hence what sentences or propositions constitute the argument mirrored or embodied in these beliefs and judgments, are a matter of what that agent *takes* as providing him or her with reason to act. Depending on the agent, these might be something that he or she thinks morality requires, for instance, or helps feed hungry children overseas, or almost anything else. Independently of Davidson's point about the fact that people often reason about *conflicting* motives and purposes, it is simply not true that all (or even many) agents act on the view that only their own wants (or needs or purposes) provide them with reason to act. For those agents who do not act on this view, the premises that lead them to conclusions about what they should do, even in the simplest case when there is no conflict, may make no mention whatsoever of their own motives and how to achieve them.

Of course, one might want to know what the structure of practical reasoning *ought* to be, rather than what it is, i.e., one might want to know not what beliefs or judgments *actually* lead agents to form judgments about what they ought to do but what ones *should* lead them to such judgments. This is a question about what really does give agents good reason to act, and hence about what sorts of premises really do support (or even entail) propositions about what agents should do. This is a basic question in ethics (broadly understood). Indeed, it is the question to which Williams and Schiffer have proposed partial answers, as we have seen. But as such, is it a question that can be decided merely by investigating the *form* of practical arguments?

If, as I am assuming for the moment, the conclusion of a practical argument is always some sentence or proposition about what the agent should do or has the best reason to do or the like, then it is a substantive and highly controversial claim to hold that such propositions can be validly supported *only* if the agent has some end that he or she wants or needs or is striving for and the act in question somehow promotes or "contributes to realizing" that end. In essence, this seems to be the very same conclusion that Williams was arguing for in his internal-reasons theory of justifying reasons. But this is a large and controversial claim, and if true, it overturns much of commonsense morality, as well as many important philosophical theories of morality. It entails the denial of the claim that justice, truth, the needs of others, even one's own needs *just by themselves* ever give one reason to act. Such things will give someone a reason, on this view, only if that person already has some motive, purpose, or end that involves these things.

How can such a far-reaching and, in the end, deeply skeptical conclusion possibly be part of what one would have thought was supposed to be a humdrum account of the basic schema of practical reasoning? The practical syllogism is presented as a neutral account of the form that practical reasoning must take, not something that commits one to far-reaching and deeply skeptical conclusions in ethics. Since it does commit one to these conclusions, we should suspect, even independently of Davidson's point, that the practical syllogism is not the correct account of practical reasoning. One would naturally expect that a neutral account could be given. At the same time, the argument of the last two chapters can help us see, I think, how one could be led into the mistake of thinking that the practical syllogism does give, in a neutral way, the form that any practical reasoning must take.

My hypothesis about how this happens is this. Practical reasoning, like other sorts of reasoning, is a mental process. It involves making judgments or forming beliefs usually on the basis of other judgments or beliefs one already holds. In the case of practical reasoning, the whole point of engaging in this process is to figure out what to do, how to act. If in fact this process leads one to act (perhaps via the formation of an intention to act), then some of those beliefs or judgments, or all of them together, "motivated" one to act. That is, if in fact one acts on the basis of some piece of practical reasoning one has undertaken, then it follows that one's reason or reasons for doing what one did are contained in the practical reasoning one did. And since humans are purposive beings, this will reveal something, perhaps a lot, about the purposes of the agent doing the reasoning. So it will be natural to describe the agent's reasons, as given in his or her practical reasoning, in terms of what he or she wants to do, or has a pro attitude toward doing, or the like. And from this it will be very easy to slip into saying that the *content* of at least some of the beliefs or judgments that the agent made in the course of practical reasoning was that he or she wanted something or other to be the case, especially if one doesn't have clearly in mind the distinction between pro attitudes and desires proper. Without this distinction there will seem to be nothing wrong with moving from "The agent wants that p" and "The agent's wants are revealed in his or her practical reasoning" to "This practical reasoning must in part be about what he or she wants."

So here is at least one source of the problem. It doesn't follow at all from the fact that an agent's pro attitudes are revealed by the practical reasoning he or she does that the *content* of the judgments or beliefs involved in some piece of practical reasoning must mention the agent's purposes or wants or desires. (Nor, of course, does it follow that one specific judgment or belief must sum up all the relevant purposes involved in moving the agent to perform the action he does. I'll return in a moment to the question of how this thought comes in.) There is a great difference between saying that when one acts on the basis of practical reasoning, one's desires, motives, or (what we are calling) pro attitudes are thereby *revealed,* and saying that in the *content* of the judgments involved in this reasoning, reference must be made to one's desires. When I go to a meeting because I believe that it is my responsibility to do so, this shows that I have a pro attitude toward going. But the content of my belief is "that I have a responsibility to go," not that I have a desire to go. Only if we forget the distinction between pro attitudes and desires proper can we identify a *belief* or judgment that, by its place in someone's practical reasoning, reveals that agent's pro attitude (perhaps to some observer) with the *content* of that belief, which may or may not be about the agent's desires proper. Having thus been led not to distinguish the belief from its propositional content, we will be lead to hold that this "desire" revealed by the practical reasoning must be referred to somewhere in the content of the practical reasoning.

This seems to be what has happened in Audi's case. In the course of his argument that the practical syllogism, in the form given in the quote above, gives the "simplest basic schema for practical reasoning," Audi says, "There is wide (though not universal) agreement that the major premise expresses (possibly by explicitly reporting) some want of [the subject's], in the broad sense of 'want' encompassing any kind of motivation, extrinsic or intrinsic" (1989, 95–96). McGinn uses this same idea in an example in his discussion of the practical syllogism. He moves from saying "If my reason for boiling the kettle is to make tea, then I desire to make tea and I believe that boiling the kettle will contribute towards the satisfaction of that desire" to saying that we can represent my reasoning as a practical syllogism with "[Person] A desires to have tea" as the first premise (McGinn 1979, 23). So somehow the pro attitutde revealed by my boiling the kettle of water has come to be referred to in the content of my practical reasoning.

But there is a great difference between a judgment of mine expressing, in the sense of *revealing,* a desire or pro attitude of mine and its *reporting* one of my desires, that is, containing a reference to one of my desires as part of its propositional content. My judgment or belief that it is my duty to get you some food might figure into a piece of practical reasoning that results in my going to the grocery to buy you some food. It thus reveals my pro attitude toward getting you more food (or toward doing my duty). It does this, however, even though the content of this judgment ("It is my duty to get you some food") makes no reference to my desires or other pro attitudes at all.

If I am right in thinking that aficionados of the practical syllogism as the basic schema of practical reasoning have confused what practical reasoning reveals about the agent's desires or pro attitudes with the propositional content and argumentative structure of the judgments that do or should make up the practical reasoning, then there is a rather simple explanation of why Davidson's point about the inability of the practical syllogism to deal with conflicting reasons has been overlooked. After all, when one finally gets around to performing an action, whatever conflicts one saw among the reasons for and against performing it must have been resolved, at least in one's own mind. So what, in the course of the reasoning, may have been regarded by the agent as one among many conflicting reasons will appear, once the action has been performed, as *the* reason for which it was performed. As Davidson puts it, "What emerges, in the *ex post facto* atmosphere of explanation and justification, as *the* reason frequently was, to the agent at the time of action, one consideration among many, a reason" (1980, 16). So the error that leads to thinking that the content of the judgments involved must refer to a desire or other motive will also lead to the thought that there is only one main motive in any action. That is, it will lead to the thought that practical reasoning always involves a single major premise whose content refers to some desire or motive of the agent.

This also throws light, I think, on the dispute mentioned above between those who, like Audi, think that the conclusion of the practical syllogism is a sentence or proposition and those, like Anscombe (and apparently Aristotle), who think it is an action. If we think of the enterprise we are engaged in as a search for the agent's reason for performing whatever act he or she performs, then, of course, we will find that whenever someone acts for a reason, he or she has a desire (i.e., pro attitude) toward an action of a certain kind and believes that the action performed is of that kind. So here the "conclusion will be an action," in the sense that it is an action that is being explained. But it is a mistake to move from this, which is really nothing more than a restatement of Nagel's "entailment point" discussed in chapter 1 and is a point about the agent's reasons (explaining reasons), to any conclusion about "practical reason" in any sense in which this is supposed to tell us something about *good* reasons for performing actions.

If one makes this mistake, then one will hold the practical syllogism to be some sort of normative standard of practical reasoning with a major premise that refers to some motive of the agent's and a minor premise that describes how to accomplish whatever end is given in the major premise. This will not only involve, as I have said, the confusion of thinking of the pro attitude *revealed* in some action with a desire proper *referred to* in the major premise of this reasoning, but also, since this is *reasoning*, the conclusion will now have to be a judgment (or perhaps the propositional content of a judgment), not an action.

I can put this more sharply by saying that in the only sense in which the practical syllogism makes any sense, its "conclusion" is an action, all right, but it is not about *practical reason* at all. It is about the agent's reasons, explaining reasons. It tells us, in essence, that whenever anyone acts for a reason, he or she has a pro attitude toward an action of some kind and judges this act to be of this kind (which is Davidson's C1; see the beginning of chapter 2). In the sense in which the practical syllogism is about practical reason (that is, good reasoning about what to do, justifying reasons), its conclusion will, of course have to be a judgment (or the propositional content of a judgment), but there is just no reason at all to think that it is correct. There is no reason at all to think that agents either do or should refer to their own desires proper when deciding what to do, let alone only one per action.

THE ROLE OF DESIRES PROPER IN PRACTICAL REASON

It is time to take stock. In this chapter and the previous one, we have been looking at arguments that, their authors claim, establish a connection between desires of some sort and good or justifying reasons for acting. One of these arguments, Schiffer's, focused clearly on a variety of what I have called desires proper, namely r-p desires, and tried to establish that having such a desire was sufficient for having a good reason to act to satisfy it. I argued that this is correct only if we accept the specific analysis of r-p desires as having the phenomenological character of being automatically pleasurable to satisfy, and accept the (I think plausible) additional principle that one has reason to perform any action that will bring one pleasure or relieve discomfort. This means, however, that it is the prospect of pleasure, not the desire itself, that gives one a reason to satisfy such an r-p desire.

The other sort of argument, exemplified by the doctrine that practical reasoning always does or should take the form of a practical syllogism as well as by Williams's internal-reasons account of justifying reasons, holds that a necessary condition of having a good reason to act is that one have a desire, in some sense of this term. This claim, I have argued, is only plausible if we understand "desire" in what I have called the pro-attitude sense. But since from the fact that one intentionally performed some action it follows that one had a pro attitude of some sort toward doing whatever it was that one was trying to achieve, this is not a condition with which even the most severe externalist should be unhappy. It is only if one confuses pro attitudes with desires proper—and so thinks that this requirement somehow shows that considerations of justice, say, or the needs of others, or the like, can't all by themselves give anyone any reason to act—that externalism would be under any threat. But the claim that a necessary condition of having a good reason to act is that one have a desire proper to do so gets no support at all from the sorts of explanatory and motivational considerations cited in favor of the internal-reasons theory and the practical syllogism.

Nor does it seem independently plausible. If I am weighing my strong desire to stay home and read against my responsibility to go to a meeting at my son's school, a responsibility that I believe I have and believe I ought to follow but feel no proper desire to follow, this sort of doctrine, by itself, will reveal no dilemma, no conflict, here at all. If I have no desire to go to the meeting or to fulfill my responsibilities, then, on such a view, I have no reason to do so either. But if, as seems obvious, there is a genuine conflict of reasons in such a situation, then any view that takes having a desire proper as a necessary condition for having a justifying reason to act must be mistaken.

At the same time, however, it is at least not obvious that anything I have said so far shows a dilemma or conflict of reasons in such a situation either, even if we assume that one always has reason to do what one has a responsibility to do. This is because nothing I have said so far makes sense of the idea that usually, at least, we have reason to do what will satisfy our desires proper. One might, I suppose, try to claim that my desire to stay home and read is an r-p desire of the sort explained in this chapter or, perhaps more plausibly, that it is a motivated desire for the pleasure of staying home and reading (again I assume that one has reason to do what will bring one pleasure). But even if one of these two views is correct in this case, this doesn't solve the wider problem.

After all, both Schiffer's idea of r-p desires and the practical syllogism (considered as an account of justifying reasons) seemed plausible originally because it seems plausible to think that, at least when other things are equal, one's own desires give one reason to act to satisfy them. And nothing said so far either explains this idea or explains it away. Here is a suggestion that, though it does nothing to resurrect the practical syllogism, is at least consistent with the above account of r-p desires and makes some sense of the broader idea that, other things being equal, desires proper provide us with reasons to act to satisfy them.

It is common in moral philosophy to distinguish actions that are forbidden, actions that are required, and actions that are neither, i.e., actions where one is permitted to do as one chooses. Some versions of act-consequentialism, for instance, have come under attack for not making room for actions one is neither forbidden from performing nor required to perform (see, for instance, Scheffler 1982). My suggestion is simply that something like this distinction applies in practical rationality generally, in the following way. There are or at least seem to be some "things" (let me leave it as vague as this for the moment) that one always has reason to seek or avoid, because, so to speak, of what they are. Justice, for instance, might be such a thing, but we don't have to think of these things as states of affairs to be produced. It could be that one always has reason not to lie, for instance. But we need not think of these things as having moral or interpersonal value, since, I would suppose, one paradigm case of something one always has good reason to promote is one's own good (see McDowell 1978). Perhaps another such paradigm case would be that one always has good reason to avoid one's own pain.

In general, it would appear, desires proper don't much enter into the story of things that are automatically reason-providing. One has reason to get or promote or try to achieve such things (assuming that there really are reason-providing things) not because one has a desire for them but because of what they are. This is the point over which Schiffer's r-p desires stumbled. If, as I have explained them, at least, r-p desires are always and automatically pleasurable to satisfy, then it would seem that for all that has been said so far, it can just be the fact that I will get some pleasure that gives me reason to satisfy my r-p desires, rather than the fact that such r-p desires are desires or have the sorts of features discussed above. And my own pleasure would seem to be one of the "things" I always have reason to promote.

I will call reasons of the sort I am describing "objective" reasons, but there could be such reasons even if only my own needs, say, give me reason to act, that is, even if nothing independent of me gives me reason to do anything. My need for water might give me such an objective reason to try to get some water, but it is another question whether it gives you any reason to help me get some. Objective reasons in this sense contrast with what I will call "permissible" reasons. Many purposes, goals, projects, and the like that people have in their lives, though they are in some sense open to choice, are not ones that can themselves be justified by reference to anything further, whether universal justice or simply the self-interest of the agent in question. If I have a need for water, then presumably I have reason to want to get it, and we might even want to hold that others have reason to help me get it. But, to use Nagel's example (1986, 167), if I badly want to climb to the top of Mount Kilimanjaro, that doesn't mean that others have reason to help me do so. Nor does it mean that I have any reason to climb Mount Kilimanjaro *other than the fact that I want to.*

If I need water, not only do I have reason to try to get it, I also have reason to want to get it. My desire for water is itself justified by my need for water. So my reason is objective. But there may be nothing about climbing Mount Kilimanjaro that gives me reason to do so or to want to do so. It may just be something that I want to do. In such a situation, I am suggesting, I will have reason to climb the mountain just because I want to do so. My reason for doing so will be permissible. So the suggestion that there are permissible reasons, as well as objective reasons, can be put by saying that not only are there things that practical reason (or maybe Reason with a capital "R") requires and forbids that one consider when one is deliberating about what to do, but there are also other things one is allowed to consider or not, and among these are the "objects" of ones own desires proper. Objective reasons, if they exist, are things we must take into account in practical deliberation. Permissible reasons are things we may take into account. There may be nothing at all to be said for my climbing to the top of Mount Kilimanjaro before I come to want to do so. But once I have this desire, there is nothing irrational about regarding this as a reason to make this climb. Reason permits me to do so.

This suggestion (which follows Nagel 1986, chap. 9) that we distinguish objective from permissible reasons mirrors, as I said, the distinction in morals and the law between, on the one side, things we are required or forbidden to do and, on the other side, things we are permitted to do or not as we choose. Objective reasons, if there are such, are based on things we always have some reason to do or avoid. Permissible reasons exist typically because an agent has some desire proper. So the suggestion I am making here is, we might say, about the structure of practical reason. Even if it is accepted, of course, this suggestion leaves lots of questions unanswered. There is the obvious question of how justice, or even self-interest for that matter, can actually provide anyone with an objective reason. And there is also the question of how we are to weigh the two sorts of reasons against each other when they conflict. (On this, see Nagel 1986, chap. 9, and Scanlon 1975.)

But, I think, this suggestion does let us get some perspective on many of the claims about justifying reasons that I have surveyed in this chapter and the last, including the status of whims, which I think we can regard as desires proper (with perhaps odd or frivolous objects) that do not connect to any of the agent's plans, interests, or the like. (They will thus provide [perhaps weak] permissible reasons to act on them.) The idea that a necessary condition of having a good reason to do something is that one have a desire proper that the action in question will somehow contribute to satisfying is an idea that seems involved both in Williams's internal-reasons theory and in the practical syllogism. The suggestion I am making here lets us see their positions as holding that all reasons have the structure of permissible reasons, that is, as denying that there are any objective reasons at all.

Exactly the opposite mistake, or at least assumption, lies behind Schiffer's account of r-p desires. If the idea that there are permissible reasons makes sense, then any, or at least most, desires can give one reason to act to satisfy them. There is no need to try to find any special "internal" structure of the sort Schiffer proposes for r-p desires in order for desires to be reason-providing. So it would seem that only if one thought that all reasons for acting were objective reasons would one think that a special, self-reflective connection with pleasure was needed for a desire to be reason-providing.

In this chapter and the last we have been looking at the role desires play in justifying reasons for action. From the next chapter the focus shifts to a quite different issue: the role of desires in explanations of action.

4   Desires in the Explanation of Actions: Part 1, Desires as Causes of Action

We have been looking in the last two chapters at how desires have been thought to figure in the rational justification of actions. In this and the next chapter the subject changes. In chapter 2, I distinguished Davidson's explanatory version of the desire/belief model of reasons from Williams's internal-reasons version, which was an account of justifying reasons. I went on, in that chapter and in chapter 3, to criticize the justifying-reasons version. In this chapter I want to begin to examine how desires figure in explanations of action. One way in which they might do this, a way famously defended by Davidson, is by somehow being the causes of the actions that they explain.

According to W. D. Hart, "The grounds for thinking that the relation between beliefs and desires, on the one hand, and bodily actions that they explain, on the other, is causal are the same as the grounds for distinguishing a person's real reasons that are not good from good reasons that are not really his, that is, rationalizations of what he does, by saying that the first, but not the second, causes him to do what he does; no other way to make the distinction clear seems known" (1988, 169).

This reasoning seems to me to be "too quick." It is clear that there is a distinction between explaining reasons and justifying reasons. My reason for taking the bus to campus this morning (I needed to get here quickly) might not be a good reason (it is actually faster to come by bike). And equally, my reason for taking the bus might be a crummy one, even though I also have a good reason to do so, a reason on which, however, I do not act. Such explanations of actions in terms of the agent's reasons, I assume, are genuinely explanatory, at least sometimes. But unless one takes "*a* causes *b*" to mean nothing more than "*a* explains *b*," in which case, of course, all explanations (that involve whatever sorts of things *a* and *b* are supposed to be) will be "causal" of necessity, it is an extra step to say that the explanation involved in referring to an agent's reasons is a causal explanation.

The question of whether an agent performed some action *because* he or she had some desire can frequently be given an affirmative answer if we are speaking of desires proper, and it can always be affirmatively answered if we are speaking of pro attitudes. Even when I dutifully trudge off to that meeting only because I believe I have a responsibility to do so, still, the fact that I went voluntarily shows that I wanted to go (in the pro-attitude sense of "want"), and hence it is not incorrect, even if not very informative, to say that I went because I wanted to. (Pointing this out might be a way of underlining the fact that I went voluntarily; nobody forced me to go.) But this only shows how very broadly "because" can be used. It certainly does not show that explanations of actions in terms of the agent's pro attitudes are causal explanations in any of the stronger or more restricted senses in which philosophers have used this term.

"Because" is simply one of the most general terms by which we mark explanatory claims. And there seem to be plenty of forms of explanation that are not obviously causal. Explaining why a player moved a piece as he did in a chess match, someone might say, "Black didn't attack white's rook by moving his queen's pawn, because that would put his own king in check from the white king's bishop." This might be a genuine, even enlightening explanation either of black's actual move or of his failure to attack white's rook to someone who either hadn't noticed that black's moving his queen's pawn would result in his own king being placed in check or did not know the rule forbidding such moves. But, especially in the latter case, where we explain why a move was made or another not made by saying it was because the rules required or forbad the move, it certainly doesn't look much like a causal explanation. Or, just to have another example, consider the math teacher who explains to his or her class that 12 is the square root of 144 because multiplying 12 times 12 gives 144.

So if we are interested in the question of whether explanations of actions in terms of the agent's pro attitudes are causal explanations, we need to specify some stronger, more restricted notion of causal explanation than simply an explanation that legitimately uses the term "because." "Because" applies to virtually all genuine explanations, and so cannot be used to distinguish causal explanations from any other variety. At the same time, it is crucial to keep in mind that the sorts of explanation we are focusing on are ones that cite pro attitudes in the course of giving the agent's reason or reasons for doing whatever he or she did. That is, these explanations use as an essential feature the fact that the agent conceived of the action in a way that made it appear somehow attractive, at least to him or her and at the time the act was performed or the decision to perform it was made. As Davidson puts it, "From the agent's point of view there was, when he acted, something to be said for the action" (1980, 9).

In other words, explanations of actions in terms of the agent's pro attitudes explain the action in question partly by the fact that the agent conceived of it in a certain way.

And this fact itself figures essentially into the explanation. So if such explanations are to be causal, this semantic feature of the explanations will have to get a causal analysis. "The fact that [beliefs and pro attitudes] have a content, the fact that they have a *semantic* character, must be relevant to the kind of effects they produce," as Fred Dretske (1988, 80) says. "If brain structures possessing meaning affect motor output in the way the soprano's acoustic productions affect glass, then the meaning of these neural structures is causally inert. Even if it is there, it doesn't *do* anything."

In this chapter we will be examining attempts by Alvin Goldman and by Dretske himself to give a causal account of just this feature of explanations of action. In terms of the distinction drawn in chapter 2 between the two different sorts of desire/belief models, explanatory and justificatory, both Goldman and Dretske are attempting to give a causal account of how the explanatory version of the desire/belief model of an agent's reasons succeeds in explaining actions. I will raise some doubts about whether either manages to accomplish this task. But the more important point to see here, I will suggest, is that there is a distinctive, and extremely difficult, *kind* of problem that any causal analysis of desire/belief explanations faces.

GOLDMAN'S ANALYSIS OF DESIRE/BELIEF EXPLANATIONS

We may begin by looking at Goldman's well-known causal account of explanation of action. Goldman (1970, 57) makes it part of his analysis of the concept of "intentional-act token" that it is caused by beliefs and desires "in a certain characteristic way." Likewise, "The concept of wanting is the concept of something that tends to have certain effects, viz. acts." So, according to him, "it is a *logical* truth about wants that they tend to *cause* acts" (Goldman 1970, 112). Thus there is no question, for Goldman, of whether desires cause actions. On his view, both concepts, act and desire, have the idea of causal connection built into them as a matter of their meaning.

The second main feature of desires that Goldman's theory needs to make sense of the explanatory force of the desire/belief model is a connection between desires and rational deliberation. This is contained in Goldman's account of occurrent wants, which get explained in terms of their contrast with standing wants.

An occurrent want [he says] is a mental event or mental process; it is a "going on" or "happening" in consciousness. A standing want . . . is a disposition or propensity to have an occurrent want, a disposition that lasts with the agent for a reasonable length of time. Though it is perhaps theoretically possible for a person to have such a disposition without ever having any manifestations thereof, we would not ascribe such a disposition to anyone unless the relevant manifestations appeared from time to time. (Goldman 1970, 86)

The term "standing want" is something of a misnomer here, since, strictly speaking, on Goldman's view, the dispositions he calls "standing wants" are not dispositions to act but rather dispositions to have occurrent wants, which do all the causal work. "Standing wants and beliefs," he says (1970, 88), "can affect actions only by becoming activated, that is, by being manifested in occurrent wants." Thus "the role of causing actions must be assigned to occurrent wants and beliefs, not standing ones." At the same time, one is always, so to speak, automatically aware of one's occurrent wants. "To have an *occurrent* want is to have an *occurrent* thought of X as attractive, nice, good, etc. a favorable regarding, viewing or taking of the prospect of X" (Goldman 1970, 94). "It is part of our notion of an ordinary (occurrent) desire that an agent is aware of this desire" (p. 98).

So Goldman holds that practical inference is "where a person comes to have a certain want on the basis of some combination of other wants and beliefs" (p. 100). "Wants lead to basic acts via a series of practical inferences," he says, "in which an agent's beliefs and perhaps additional wants come into play" (p. 114). The principle that governs these practical inferences, Goldman calls "L'":

If any agent S believes that hypothetical act-tree $A_1, A_2, \ldots,$ A_n (to be performed at t) is more likely, all in all, to achieve more of his desires than any other act-tree (that could be performed at t), and if S is in standard conditions with respect to each of his basic acts of this act-tree (at t), then S performs each of these basic acts (at t). (Goldman 1970, 74)

In Goldman's terminology, a basic act is one that one can perform "at will," such as moving one's finger, while an "act tree" is the set of what Goldman regards as distinct acts "generated" by such a basic act, e.g., flipping the switch, turning on the light, illuminating the room, wasting electricity, alerting the prowler that one is home.[1] "Standard conditions" include not being physically unable to perform the act in question, not already being in the state to which the act in question involves changing, and the like (Goldman 1970, 65).

So desires in this model, that is, occurrent desires in Goldman's account, have two very different features: they do the (allegedly causal) "work" in producing actions, and they are automatically open to conscious awareness. And, of course, it is this second feature that allows them to take part in rational deliberation. But there is a puzzle here. On the one side, L' is presented as at least a first stab at an actual law. Under certain conditions, "S performs" certain acts, it says. On the other side, it is clear from Goldman's discussion of L' that its success at predicting or explaining action will depend completely on how S deliberates, i.e., weighs up his or her various desires and beliefs in deciding what to do. On this subject, Goldman says that how well L' works "depends in part on what sort of decision 'criterion' the agent employs" (p. 74). So if, for instance, S had and used some very eccentric weighing principle for his or her desires, or perhaps even simply didn't regard such desires as important in deliberation at all, L' would, or at least might, fail completely. But what sort of "causal law" is it (no matter how "rough" or "preliminary" in form) that depends in this way on the "decision criterion" that the agent involved selects? Will we need other principles, totally unlike L' perhaps, for agents who select different criteria?

The difficulty is, I would say, that L' tries to see desires as being involved in two radically different explanatory schemas. That is, it tries to see desires *both* as things about which an agent can deliberate (and hence as things that can be ignored, things about which the agent can be mistaken, and the like, in short, what I have called desires proper) *and* as the basic explanatory factors (possibly even, as Goldman holds, causal ones) in explanations or predictions of behavior (that is, as what I have called pro attitudes).

These two features fit together in a single concept only very badly. In fact, it is hard to see that they fit together at all, which was why each was assigned a different label in chapter 1. If it is the deliberative process that explains the resulting action, then it is not the desire (proper), with its alleged causal powers, that is essential to the explanation but rather the agent's awareness of it, that is, the agent's belief or judgment that he or she has this desire. The same explanation would work even if the agent *wrongly* judged that he or she had some desire. (This will be true even if one holds that such inconvenient mistakes are never actually made for some reason, perhaps because, as Goldman holds, we are always somehow automatically aware of our occurrent desires.) Alternatively, if it is the causal powers *of the desire itself* that, in the presence of the requisite beliefs, explain the resulting action, then it is hard to see why awareness of it, or judgments about it, should be needed. Why shouldn't my mere desire for coffee, whether or not I also judge that I have this desire, combine with my belief that there is coffee in the kitchen to get me moving in that direction?

A glance at L' itself will show that, as I said, Goldman actually opts for the former, deliberative explanatory schema, since he says in L' that if any agent *believes* that some act is more likely to achieve more of his or her desires than any other act, then the agent performs this act. So what are important here are not the agent's actual desires but rather what the agent believes about his or her desires, which is, of course, what is required if the agent's reasoning about his or her desires is to play the central role Goldman wants it to play. What this means, however, is that the "causal analysis" of the desire/belief model of action explanation supposed to be contained in Goldman's theory is simply a sham. The "causal powers" of desires to produce actions, which Goldman builds into them by definition, work in this theory *only* via the fact that agents make judgments about their own desires, judgments that then figure into rational deliberation that eventually results in action. If *this* is the sense in which desires cause actions, then there is no difference between desires and anything else that a deliberating agent might make judgments about in the course of deliberating about what to do. Even totally nonexistent beings, such as Santa Claus and the Easter Bunny, can and do have this sort of causal influence on actions.

None of this, of course, shows that L' is itself in any way defective as a principle for explaining actions, since it might be that agents always do deliberate and act on the desires they believe they have in just the way L' says. Whether it or principles like it work to explain actions via the deliberation of the agent involved will be discussed below in chapter 5. The point here is that if we are going to have a causal analysis, in any interesting sense, of how the desire/belief model explains actions, the causal feature of the analysis can't simply assume the deliberative process as an element and then let this essentially unanalyzed feature do all the explanatory work. If it does, then the "desires" to which it is attributing causal powers have these powers only in virtue of the judgments the deliberating agent makes about them.

The complaint I am making against Goldman's view can be put succinctly in the terminology adopted in chapter 1 by saying that Goldman has attempted to give a causal account of the way in which the desire/belief model of explanatory reasons explains actions that focuses on desires proper, that is, desires in the sense in which it is possible to act even when one has no proper desire at all to do what one intentionally does. This is why L' might not even apply if the agent whose action is being explained chooses a "decision criterion" that doesn't even involve looking at his or her own desires, i.e., at his or her desires proper. This is to say, desires proper very often explain actions only via the judgments agents make about them in the course of deliberation. A causal account of how desires explain actions therefore needs at the very least to focus on desires in the sense in which any judgment, even a false judgment about what I have a proper desire for, counts as a "desire" if it leads me to act; that is, it needs to focus on pro attitudes. In essence this is what Fred Dretske has recently tried to do. So it is to his account I now turn.

Dretske, like Goldman, is giving an account of the desire/ belief model of explanatory reasons. He holds that "*both* belief (or some cognitive variant thereof) and desire (or some conative variant thereof) are operative in everything we do that is explicable by means of an agent's reasons" (Dretske 1988, 109). And he makes clear that he is using "desire" in what I have labeled the pro-attitude sense. His basic idea is that "when we seek an explanation of behavior in terms of the agent's reasons, we are . . . always looking for a structuring cause [of that behavior]" (Dretske 1988, 50). We will need to examine the details of how this claim gets spelled out, but the rough idea of a "structuring cause" can be given in terms of any instrumentally purposive device, such as a thermostat, to take Dretske's own example.

When the temperature in my house drops below the assigned level then, if the thermostat is working correctly, the furnace gets switched on. What Dretske calls the "triggering cause" of the furnace going on is the temperature in the house dropping below the assigned level. Knowing the triggering cause, we know why the thermostat switched on the furnace when it did. But, of course, exactly this same mechanical device might have been wired up to something other than my furnace. It might have been wired up to your furnace or to my garage door or to nothing at all. We learn nothing about why it was wired up to produce this particular causal sequence, starting my furnace rather than some other furnace or none at all, when we learn the triggering cause. The answer to this sort of question—why did it produce this causal sequence rather than some other one—will describe what Dretske calls the structuring cause.

Of course, in the case of the thermostat attached to my furnace, the structuring cause of why it turns on my furnace when the temperature in my house falls below the assigned point, rather than opening my garage door, say, will have to be given in terms of the intentions and plans of the one who originally wired the thing up. But Dretske's idea is that desires and beliefs are structuring causes of behavior and that they acquire their functions in the causal sequence (which *is* the behavior) from learning and reinforcement, rather than from someone else setting the mechanism up so that some sort of event will trigger some movement.

For Dretske, behavior is a causal process that begins with some internal event and terminates in some "product," usually movement of some sort. The triggering cause is whatever starts this process going; the structuring cause is whatever gets it to go in the way it does, rather than in some other way (Dretske 1988, chap. 2). This view of behavior is broad enough to apply even to trees dropping their leaves in autumn. It makes sense of the idea that this is something trees *do*. But in the case of humans' and some animals' behavior of some kinds, the structuring causes will be desires and beliefs.

The difficult question here, which Dretske faces up to squarely, is how internal states or events of some organism that are supposed to be, under one description, merely the initial events in a causal process that has, say, some bodily movement as its terminal event or product can be, under another description, contentful in the way in which beliefs, desires, and other such intentional states are supposed to be. Such states are intentional; that is, beliefs are *about* things, and desires are *for* things, to put it as vaguely as possible. So the question is how to explain these causal sequences in such a way as to make sense of and justify these intentional descriptions. Dretske gives roughly parallel answers for beliefs and desires, but since I wish to concentrate on the latter, I will give only a brief sketch of the answer he gives for beliefs.

Some states or events "indicate" things, according to Dretske, just because they are in certain causal relations to them. The tracks in the snow indicate deer because only deer make tracks of that shape. This is what H. P. Grice (1957) called "natural meaning." "Indicators" in this sense cannot be wrong. If the tracks really indicate deer, then there must be deer around. We sometimes, according to Dretske, "recruit" such straightforward causal indicators for our own purposes. When we do, we give something that, by its causal connections, naturally indicates various things, the function of indicating one thing in particular, and thus the function of "representing" this thing in such a way that what is represented might not be the case. This is an essential element of genuine, nonnatural meaning.

> If a full tank of gas means (because of the weight of the gas) that there is a large downward force on the bolts holding the tank to the car's frame, then the fuel gauge indicates a large downward force on these bolts whenever it indicates a full tank of gas. In addition, electrically operated fuel gauges indicate not only the amount of fuel left in the tank but also the amount of electrical current flowing in the wires connecting the gauge to the tank, the amount of torque on the armature to which the pointer is affixed, and the magnitude of the magnetic field surrounding this armature. Given the way these gauges operate, they cannot indicate (i.e., have their behavior depend on) the amount of fuel in the tank without indicating (exhibiting at least the same degree of dependency on) these related conditions. Nevertheless, we take one of these indicated conditions to be what the gauge *represents*. (Dretske 1988, 59)

> What a system *represents* is *not* what its (expressive) elements indicate or [naturally] mean. It is what these elements have the *function* of indicating or meaning. (P. 59)

Its *representational* efforts—and therefore its representational failures, its *mis*representations—are limited to what it has the function of indicating. (P. 60)

In this sort of case, of course, this representational function is assigned by us (or by the manufacturer) to what is already a natural indicator of the level of gas in the tank. (It is "natural" in the sense that, because of the way the gauge is wired up, the needle pointing in this direction indicates that the tank is full in the same way in which the tracks in the snow indicate deer.) Once we assign the needle the function of indicating the fuel level, it then "represents" the fuel level, and if there is a foul-up, it can misrepresent it. Dretske's claim about beliefs is, in essence, that they are a variety of "natural systems of representation," that is, of systems "which have *their own* intrinsic indicator functions, functions that derive from the way the indicators are developed and used *by the system of which they are a part*" (p. 62). In particular, beliefs are natural indicators that have acquired, through learning, the function of causing certain movements. Hence the fact that they are indicators explains the fact that they cause the movements they do. If some brain state, say, is caused in some animal by the sight (sound, smell, etc.) of one of its predators (and so naturally indicates that predator) and, after a few nasty encounters, this brain state comes to produce some form of escape behavior in the animal, then this natural indicator has acquired the function of representing the predator to the animal. Being in this brain state could cause the animal to run away even if, on some occasion, the brain state was not actually produced by the presence of the predator. "A belief," Dretske says, "is merely an indicator whose natural meaning has been converted into a form of non-natural meaning by being given a job to do in the explanation of behavior" (p. 84).

So on Dretske's view,

> The idea will be that during the normal development of an organism, certain internal structures *acquire* control over peripheral movements of the systems of which they are a part. Furthermore, the explanation, or part of the explanation, for this assumption of control duties is not (as in the case of artifacts) what anyone *thinks* these structures mean or indicate but what, in fact, they *do* mean or indicate about the external circumstances *in which* these movements occur and *on which* their success depends. In the process of acquiring control over peripheral movements (in virtue of what they indicate), such structures acquire an indicator function and, hence, the capacity for misrepresenting how things stand. This, then, is the origin of genuine meaning and, at the same time, an account of the respect in which this meaning is made relevant to behavior. (P. 88)

It may be wondered how a theory of belief based in this way on natural indicators, that is, on direct causal connections between the things indicated and the states that do the indicating, could ever make sense of beliefs about things to which no one has ever had any causal connection, negative numbers, say, or justice (or, for that matter, Santa Claus). Since I want to concentrate on what Dretske says about desire, however, I am just going to set aside worries of this sort and assume for the sake of this discussion that this account of belief is acceptable.

DRETSKE'S CAUSAL ANALYSIS OF DESIRE/BELIEF EXPLANATIONS

The account of desire that Dretske gives employs a connection between desire and some sort of reinforcement roughly analogous to the connection between a belief and the external event or object that it naturally indicates. The idea is that frequently an organism will be in a state that represents some external object or event, e.g., food, without that state, by itself, causing any behavior. The further element needed is what Dretske calls "the receptivity of an organism relative to [some] outcome." "The effectiveness of . . . food, say, . . . as a reinforcer, its effectiveness in modifying behavior, depends on the organism's occupying [a state of receptivity for food]" (Dretske 1988, 100). Such states, Dretske says, are

> *pure* desires, and they are desires *for* whatever condition or outcome they make the organism receptive to. There are as many different (pure) desires as there are distinguishable states of receptivity (i.e., states of receptivity for different things). Other desires—what I shall call (cognitively) *derived* desires—are generated by beliefs about what will secure the objects of *pure* (and other derived) desires. Without pure desires, though, there would be no desire at all, and hence no motivation, no purpose, no behavior explicable in terms of an agent's *reasons*. (P. 111)

Such pure desires, then, are states of receptivity for whatever it is that allows them to serve as reinforcers of behavior. That is, they allow us to make sense of the idea that the animal *learns* to behave in a certain way because such behavior leads to whatever it has a pure desire for.

> Think of an organism learning to do something in a specific set of conditions: it learns to produce [movement] M in conditions F by having the rewards R for producing M contingent on M's production *in F*. As we saw . . . , such a process will result in the recruitment of an F-indicator as an internal cause of M. We have labeled this internal indicator [belief] B. So, if learning is successful, B is enlisted as a partial cause of M. Since [pure desire] D is the internal state on which R's effectiveness as a reinforcer depends, successful learning also requires the animal to occupy state D when movements M are produced. R will not be effective in promoting the production of M unless the organism is in *both* state B and state D. Since M doesn't lead to R except in $F,$ and since R isn't reinforcing unless D, learning requires that *both* F and D exist for the

production of *M*. Since this is so, *R* will recruit, as a cause of *M*, both *B* and *D*. Or, if you please, the occurrence of *R* will recruit *B* as a cause of *M* only if *B* is accompanied by *D*. . . . Hence, this kind of learning results in the recruitment of *B* and *D* as *partial* or *contributory* causes of *M*.

   . . . *D* becomes a cause of *M* *because M* results in *R*. Given [that goal-directed behavior is not only behavior that tends to have a certain result but behavior that occurs *because* it tends to have this result (p. 111)], this implies that *M*'s production by *D* and *B* is goal-directed, that the behavior has *R* as its goal. It implies, in other words, that such behavior can be *explained* by facts about *B* and *D*—the facts, namely, that *B* indicates or means that condition *F* exists (that is why *it* was recruited as a partial cause of *M*) and the fact that *D* is *for R* (that is why *it* was enlisted as a partial cause of *M*). The animal behaves that way because it believes that *F* exists and wants *R*. (Pp. 112–113)

In short, on Dretske's account, we can explain the behavior of some animal in terms of its beliefs and desires, in the simplest cases at least, because the desire in question is a pure desire, a state of receptivity for something (such as food) that has come through an earlier causal process to produce precisely this behavior *just because* this behavior results in whatever this pure desire is a desire *for*, and it does this in this particular circumstance just because this sort of external circumstance is represented by one of its beliefs as now occurring. So the clearest case to which we can apply Dretske's account will be, as he himself points out (pp. 115–122), the psychology-laboratory situation where a rat, say, learns to press a bar to get food when a colored light goes on. Here during training whatever it is in the rat's brain that naturally indicates such things as colored lights will get "recruited" as a representation of the light being on through the connection with a reinforcer, food, but this connection only works because, and when, the rat is in a natural state of receptivity for food, i.e., when it is hungry. The natural indicator state and the natural receptivity state come to have certain functions, and hence to be a belief and a desire, by being recruited during the learning process as a causal sequence that goes from the rat's seeing the light to its pressing the bar via its having this belief and desire.

There is a question here, as Dretske is perfectly well aware (pp. 119–121), of whether the terms "belief" and "desire" are appropriately used for organisms that have such a skimpy set of them. If virtually the only interaction the rat ever has with metal bars, food pellets, colored lights, and the like is in the laboratory situation just mentioned, and this constitutes the only justification we ever have for attributing to it beliefs and desires about bars, food pellets, colored lights, and the like, then it seems to be a very large leap to say that it believes, say, that when the light goes on pressing the bar will produce food. So we may not want to use the terms "belief" and "desire" here.

The narrow dispositions to which implicit beliefs [of the sort so far described] give expression [Dretske admits] may be too narrow for the purpose of capturing our common and familiar idea of purposive, intentional, goal-directed behavior. If this is so, then we must reserve these labels for behavior that is not only goal-directed in the present sense but is also goal-*intended*—behavior that is the expression of fully explicit internal representations, and hence internal structures that have, in virtue of their content, a more versatile role in the production of output [behavior]. According to this classificatory decision, then, genuine purposive behavior will be constituted by movements, M, that have as their cause not only a B (of conditions F) and a D (for result R), but an explicit representation (some internal structure having the function of indicating) that M tends to yield R in conditions F. (P. 121)

The difference between implicit and explicit representations, as Dretske explains it, is essentially a difference in narrowness and breath of application. An implicit belief, he says, "is something like what Ryle called a single-track disposition" of a certain sort, namely, in this case, to do or believe something, given other desires and beliefs (p. 117). That is, "implicit beliefs have a content with a very narrow range of application" (p. 118). In contrast, "explicit beliefs can enter into combination with other beliefs to generate a wide range of different actions. They are potentially limitless in their application" (p. 118). But since the problem that this appeal to explicitness and implicitness of beliefs is supposed to solve is itself a problem of narrowness of the application of the "beliefs" being attributed to, in the example, the rat who pushes the bar when the light goes on, it is not clear that explaining the difference between explicit and implicit beliefs in terms of their breadth and narrowness gets Dretske very far. It may be a way of labeling the difficulty here rather than solving it. This is an issue that I am going simply to set aside for the moment, however, since it is clear that Dretske thinks that the essential elements of a causal account of agents' reasons as constituted by their desires and beliefs are contained in the explanation summarized here in the last few pages. We will need to return below to this issue of the explicitness of the beliefs involved in Dretske's explanations.

THE REWARD THESIS

A striking difference between Dretske's causal theory of beliefs and desires and Goldman's is that Dretske's account doesn't contain, and apparently doesn't need to contain, anything even remotely analogous to the principle Goldman calls L'. And if, as I have suggested, we set aside for the moment the problem about explicitness of beliefs and merely focus on the central elements of Dretske's account, there is also nothing analogous to the feature of what

Goldman calls "occurrent desires" that makes those who have them automatically aware of them (i.e., what in Goldman's account looks very like direct awareness of one's own desires). Both these differences, I think, stem from the fact that unlike Goldman's account, where the explanatory apparatus contains the rational deliberation of the agent as an essential element, Dretske's theory in its clearest and most straightforward version requires no such appeal to the deliberation of the agent whose action is being explained. If this is right, it means that Dretske's theory, at least as it applies to the simplest cases (an important qualification, as we will see below), is not subject to the objection made above to Goldman's view, i.e., that its alleged "causal" analysis of desire/belief explanations is just a sham because all the real explanatory work is done by appealing to how the agent in question reasons about his or her own desires.

There is, however, a different problem. Dretske's account, as I hope I have been able to make clear in the brief summary of it given here, depends essentially on organisms having, so to speak, certain natural desires, which he calls "pure desires" and which "are desires *for* whatever condition or outcome they make the organism receptive to" (Dretske 1988, 111). Such pure desires in Dretske's account of desire are, as I said, analogous to natural indicators in his account of belief, and they are absolutely essential because without them there could be no reinforcement, and hence no learning of whatever behavior leads to acquiring whatever the pure desire is a "receptivity state" for. "Without pure desires . . . there would be no desire at all, and hence no motivation, no purpose, no behavior explicable in terms of an agent's *reasons*" (p. 111). This is because without such pure desires there would be no reinforcement, that is, behavior wouldn't get modified because it led to whatever the pure desire was a desire for. Hence behavior couldn't be explained as taking place *because* the agent had this desire.

On the face of it, such a view commits Dretske to the thesis that all purposive behavior (or at least all behavior explainable in terms of the agent's reasons, if this is different) is undertaken, ultimately at least, to satisfy some pure desire or desires, that is, to get one or another "reinforcing result," as he puts it (p. 111). Put more starkly, Dretske seems committed to what I will call the reward thesis, that is, to the thesis that all purposive behavior is undertaken to get some "reward" (such as food, water, sex, or the like) or perhaps just pleasure (or avoidance of pain, which would presumably also have to be included). This is a version of psychological hedonism.

> The number of different pure desires will vary depending on how one identifies the reinforcing result [Dretske says]. If one identifies [result] R with external stimuli (e.g., food, water, warmth, sex) of the kinds that, as we like to say, bring pleasure, then one will have a different pure desire for each such result. If, however, one identifies R with the internal state (pleasure? need reduction?) that such different stimuli produce, one will presumably have fewer pure desires—perhaps, even, *one* pure desire: the desire for pleasure (need reduction, equilibrium, or whatever). . . . I have no interest in legislating about this issue. It is enough (for my purposes) if there is at least *one* pure desire—as indeed there must be if learning of the sort now in question is to occur. (P. 111, n. 2)

From this there would seem to be little doubt that Dretske does indeed hold that any action explainable on the basis of one or more *pure* desires is done to get, e.g., water, food, sex, pleasure, or whatever these pure desires are desires for. This doesn't quite settle the issue of whether he is committed to the reward thesis, however, because (1) Dretske holds that there are other sorts of desires than pure desires that can explain actions and (2) he might want to hold, in spite of the examples given, that pure desires can have objects other than either such "external stimuli" as food, water, sex, etc., or the "internal states," like pleasure, to which such things give rise. So we will need to examine both these points to decide whether he is really committed to the reward thesis.

The first point need not detain us long. In discussing the sorts of desire there are, Dretske says in the passage already quoted that beside pure desires there are "other desires—what I shall call (cognitively) *derived* desires—[which] are generated by beliefs about what will secure the objects of *pure* (and other derived) desires" (p. 111). From this it seems clear that the distinction between pure and derived desires is intended by Dretske to be exhaustive. And it is equally clear that any action explained by reference to derived desires is ultimately performed to get the object of some pure desire or desires, such as food, water, or whatever. And in any case, Dretske says, "Cognitively mediated desires [i.e., derived desires] . . . are explanatory artifacts. They are, so to speak, *constructions* out of the cognitive and conative elements from which they derive their goal and motivational force (hence, their explanatory efficacy)" (p. 147). So the idea that there are other sorts of desires than pure desires, since it is explained in terms of derived desires that are themselves merely logical constructs, supports, rather than argues against, the claim that Dretske is committed to some version of the reward thesis.

On the second point—whether pure desires can have objects other than food, water, sex, and the like or the internal states to which these things give rise—matters are only slightly less straightforward. So far as I can find, Dretske never directly discusses this issue except to say, in the passage quoted above (p. 111, n. 2), that he doesn't want to legislate about what the objects of pure desires have to be. He does say at one point that he does not want "to deny that one might develop a desire, a genuine, unmediated desire for something that *at first* one wanted only in a derived way or didn't want at all" (p. 148). His example is eating asparagus, which one might do at first only to please one's parents and later come to enjoy for itself. But on the same page he also says, "What I am denying, and what my account of pure desires commits me to denying, is that a pure desire can figure in the explanation of behavior if one has never experienced a gratification of that desire" (p. 148). So pure desires are the sorts of things not only that can be gratified but also whose gratification one can *experience*. Moreover, as Dretske says, if a pure desire is to explain behavior, one must *actually* have experienced this gratification. So it is hard to see how he could allow that one could have a pure desire for, say, justice. This is not because we can't experience gratification at justice being done, nor because our desire for justice can't be gratified, but because it is hard to see that having one's desire for justice gratified *need* involve any particular experience (in the way that gratification of one's desire for warmth does, say), which is what Dretske's view seems to require.

None of this quite settles the issue of what Dretske's view is here, but on the basis of the sorts of examples he gives of pure desires, as well as the way this concept figures into his theory, it certainly seems that he does have to hold that the objects of pure desires are always such things as food, warmth, sex, and the like, or the internal states to which such things give rise. (For one thing, Dretske is such a clear writer that it is hard to believe that if he had wanted to hold a view significantly different from this, he wouldn't have just flatly said so.) This is an important question because if this is indeed his view, then, as I said, he is committed to some version of the reward thesis, which is, to repeat, the thesis that every action done for a reason is ultimately to be explained by reference to the agent's desire for some reward, such as water, food, sex, or the like, or for an internal state to which such things give rise, that is, he is committed to a form of psychological hedonism. This is just a label, of course, but the problem it points to in Dretske's theory is a real one. I can put it in the terminology of chapter 1 by saying that Dretske seems committed to holding that every motivated desire, that is, every desire held for a reason, is to be explained by reference to an unmotivated desire (proper), and indeed to an unmotivated desire for one of a very restricted set of possible objects, roughly, things that bring the agent (or just plain are) pleasure or that decrease (or avoid) pain.

On this account, then, there seems to be no room for the possibility of an agent having a pro attitude that is not a proper desire at all. All motivated desires, i.e., what Dretske calls derived desires, will have to be explainable, ultimately at least, in terms of what Dretske calls pure desires, that is, in terms of unmotivated desires for food, sex, or the like, or perhaps simply to gain pleasure or avoid pain. And any action done for a reason will be explained either in terms of pure desires or derived desires. It is hard to see how Dretske, given only these materials, could possibly make sense of the idea that I might go to a meeting, for instance, and yet have no desire proper to do so, might go simply because I thought I had a responsibility to go, for example. That is, it is hard to see how he could make sense of the thought that the pro attitude on which someone acts might be a belief that the act in question has some feature that the agent thinks gives him or her a reason to act, such as that it is required by duty, or is a way of promoting the agent's interest, or the like. Since people quite frequently act on the basis of such beliefs, Dretske's account of agents' reasons cannot be correct as it stands. At the very least, something else must be added to make sense of such cases.

We get a clue to what else is needed, I think, if we look at what Dretske says (which is not much) about practical deliberation. In a section entitled "Choice, Preference, and

Decision" (pp. 138–141) Dretske provides a sketch of how he wants to deal with "behavior that is the expression of *multiple* conative and cognitive elements: desires for X competing with desires for Y, beliefs about risks being balanced against beliefs about gains, desires being modified in the light of beliefs about their means of satisfaction, and so on" (p. 138). Most of this section is given over to discussion of a case where an animal, a jackal, is faced with a situation where the only meal available, a dead antelope, is already in the possession of another animal it fears, a tiger.

The question Dretske poses is how his account deals with such a case, i.e., where the jackal has somehow to resolve two conflicting pure desires: the desire for food and the desire to avoid injury from the tiger. Each desire on its own, according to Dretske's theory, will already have been incorporated in a causal sequence that results in a specific form of behavior: eating the food when the jackal believes there is food present and is hungry and escaping when it believes there is another animal present and is afraid of being injured. By itself, each such sequence would be an example of a pure desire working in accordance with Dretske's theory as already described. But in the situation when *both* food and tiger "indicators" are present in the jackal, and hence both a pure desire to acquire food and a pure desire to avoid pain are relevant as well, a totally new form of behavior results, namely the jackal neither eats nor runs (nor both at once, of course) but waits at a safe distance hoping for leftovers.

"How this novel third result is synthesized out of control structures already available is, at the biological level, a complete mystery," Dretske says, "especially when one realizes that it may be a solution that is optimal from the point of view of securing at least partial satisfaction of both desires" (p. 141). (In fact, one might suppose that, if the jackal plays its cards right, it might *fully* satisfy both desires, i.e., it might escape injury and get a meal as well.) But Dretske doesn't regard this "complete mystery" as a counterargument to his view. According to him, his account only entails "that the jackal's behavior, however it may actually be produced, is behavior that, *if* it can be explained by what I have been calling *pure* desires (for food and the avoidance of tigers), is constituted by internal states that have had their causal roles (in the production of movement) shaped by the jackal's past commerce with tigers and food" (p. 141).

THE PROBLEM OF MULTIPLE MOTIVES

Here, finally, we can begin to make use of both the discussion earlier in this chapter of Goldman's views and the discussion in chapter 3 of the practical syllogism. Why shouldn't we simply imagine the jackal as reasoning on the basis of Goldman's principle L' (or some close analogue)? Then its behavior would not only not be a complete mystery; it would even be fairly easy to understand. The problem from Dretske's point of view would be that L' doesn't explain action in terms of what he calls pure desires; it explains them, as I argued above, in terms of beliefs or judgments *about* desires. It has to do this, since the whole force of a principle such as L' is contained in an appeal to how the agent reasons. That is, as I tried to make clear in my discussion of Goldman's supposedly causal account of how desires explain actions, importing L' into an account of the explanation of action means that all the explanatory work gets done by our notions of what it would be rational for an agent to do if it has these beliefs (including the ones about his or her own desires). Goldman's claim, then, that his is a causal account of desire/belief explanations is simply tacked on. It does no work at all in the theory itself.

The same problem will arise for Dretske's theory if it has to appeal to L' to explain the jackal's behavior (a point that, I think, Dretske's somewhat unsatisfactory discussion of explicit beliefs and desires rather conceals).

Still, I want to say, Dretske's account represents a distinct advance over Goldman's. We can see why if we recall the sort of cases where Dretske's account works, or at least comes closest to working, such as the case described above of the psychology-laboratory situation of the rat trained to press a bar to receive food when a light goes on. This sort of situation, one might say, is exactly the same one that the practical syllogism comes closest to accurately describing. There is only one desire, for food, and only one belief, that food may be had by pressing the bar now (i.e., with the light on). The idea of the practical syllogism, for instance, as it is contained in the quotation from Audi in chapter 3 above, is that it is somehow a form of *reasoning*. As I tried to show in chapter 3, considering it in this way comes to nothing. What Dretske shows, however, is that in the rather circumscribed situation of the rat pressing the bar to get food, we can understand the practical syllogism as an explanation of the action involved in straight causal terms, that is, without thinking of the animal as doing any reasoning at all.

Hence, unlike Goldman's theory, where the claim about the causal force of desires does no explanatory work at all, in the psychology-laboratory sort of case, at least, Dretske gives a sketch of a genuinely causal explanation of how what he calls "beliefs" and what he calls "desires" can combine to produce what he calls "behavior." Nothing in his account depends on anything like L', as I said, as long as we stick only to this kind of case. The difficulty comes for Dretske's account, just as it does for the practical syllogism according to Davidson, when we move to cases where there is a conflict of desires or motives of some sort.

Just as the practical syllogism provides no account of how agents should or do compare or weigh up conflicting motives, neither does Dretske's account. (Presumably, this is at least a big part of the reason why neither Dretske's theory nor the practical syllogism seems to give us much help with the idea of a good reason, as opposed to an explanatory reason; there is not enough structure in the theory to get any handle on a comparison of better and worse reasons.)

So even if we grant that Dretske's theory gives a reasonable causal account of how the desire/belief model works in the very simple psychology-laboratory case, in the *next* simplest case, such as that of the jackal, where there are only two conflicting desires or motives to be somehow resolved, it is not clear how Dretske's causal theory is supposed to work at all. It is not just that the explanation is "a complete mystery," as he says, "at the biological level." As should be clear even from the brief summary of his views given here, his theory doesn't really proceed "at the biological level." It leaves all the biology to be filled in later. The mystery is how we are supposed to extend the theory he gives for, and explains in terms of, cases of a single motive (the practical-syllogism case) to cases of multiple motives. For the former cases, the cases Dretske's theory fits, it looks as if the behavior in question resulted from reasoning in accordance with the practical syllogism (though, if Dretske is right, this appearance is misleading). In contrast, cases of multiple motives are cases where, as I suggested, it looks as if the action to be explained resulted from reasoning in accordance with Goldman's principle L'. These cases are also cases where, as I said, the problem of the explicitness of beliefs, which was set aside above, becomes even more pressing. If there is some implausibility on grounds of narrowness in saying that the causal states Dretske calls "beliefs" and "desires" are genuine beliefs and desires, even when we are dealing only with the bar-pushing rat in the psychology laboratory, this problem becomes much more acute when we are dealing with behavior such as that of the jackal in the above example, even if in the end Dretske's theory would have us say that the jackal's beliefs are also only implicit.

And, of course, this problem becomes critical in the case of some sorts of human behavior where beliefs are explicit if they ever are, namely in cases where conscious practical deliberation takes place and then an action is performed on the basis of this reasoning. That is, at the far opposite end of the spectrum of cases that starts in the psychology laboratory with a rat pushing a bar to get a food pellet whenever a light goes on are human actions where the agent consciously deliberates about what to do and then acts on the basis of his or her reasoning. Somewhere in the middle is the jackal trying to get something to eat while avoiding the tiger. The case of the human agent acting on the basis of some practical reasoning is the paradigm, presumably, of action done for a reason. And in this case, as I said, the beliefs involved are at least sometimes explicit, in the sense of being consciously formulated and employed in reasoning.

Dretske's problem of how to extend his account from the single-motive case of the psychology laboratory to the multiple-motive case of the jackal is only the first of several difficulties. In the end, if this or some similar causal account is to be successful, it will need to be able to deal with genuine practical reasoning, involving beliefs or judgments that are quite varied in content and are genuinely explicit. Since, as I have argued, human practical reasoning doesn't always involve trying ultimately to acquire water, food, sex, pleasure, or the like, it is hard to see how the account Dretske gives can possibly be expected to fit such cases. This is not to say that it doesn't fit the cases he describes or even that it can't be extended to the sort of case represented by the jackal and its conflicting desires.

Whether or not his account can be thus extended depends on whether it or some similar causal view can explain *away* the idea that the jackal is engaged in practical reasoning that uses something like Goldman's L' as its main principle. After all, if Dretske's account is successful in the simple, psychology-laboratory case of the rat pushing the bar, what it does is to make sense of the desire/belief model of explanatory reasons, for this case, without any appeal to the idea that the rat is actually doing any *reasoning,* even of the sort set out in a practical syllogism. In this simple situation the rat, we might say, behaves just as we would expect a hedonist to behave if and when he or she reasons in practical syllogisms.[2] The rat behaves, that is, just as if it had deliberated using a practical syllogism. And Dretske's theory, if it works as he wants, shows us how to do away with the "as if" in this sentence in favor of a causal explanation.

The jackal, however, can make no use of practical syllogisms, since it has more than one relevant desire. It behaves just as we would expect a hedonist to behave in such a situation if he or she reasons using Goldman's principle L'. It is probably pretty safe to assume that psychological hedonism is true of jackals—at least in the sort of situation Dretske describes—that is, that Dretske's list of rewards are the relevant ones here too. But this still leaves us with the need to give some sort of account of the causal interaction of internal states in the jackal analogous to the account Dretske gives for the bar-pushing rat if we are to do away with having to say that the jackal acts "as if it were reasoning using principle L'." Without such an account, Dretske's theory will contain an ineliminable reference to Goldman's principle L' (or some close analogue) and so will be an account no more genuinely causal for cases of multiple desires than Goldman's is for any case. (So I think Dretske is mistaken when he says that he need not give any "particular story about exactly how the [causal interaction of internal states] occurs" [1988, 141].)

Dretske's theory, as I picture it here, attempts to explain the desire/belief model of an agent's reasons by explaining *away* the appearance of genuine reasoning, substituting instead an account of how inner states of the animal in question might interact causally so as to produce the behavior we observe. Putting it this way makes it sound as if Dretske's theory could never possibly be extended to cases where there really is reasoning, that is, to at least some human cases, even independently of the commitment of this theory to psychological hedonism. But this, I think, is a mistaken view, created perhaps by the fact that we intuitively don't want to say that the rat who pushes the bar to get a food pellet is actually doing any reasoning. It is not nearly so clear that we want to say that the jackal isn't doing any reasoning. And surely a person in the jackal's situation (or rather an analogous one) might well explicitly reason out what to do and then behave in just the way the jackal does. For that matter, someone in a situation analogous to the rat in the psychology laboratory *might* explicitly reason using the relevant practical syllogism. (This seems to be the way that many advocates of the practical syllogism understand it as being used, as was argued in chapter 3 above.)

On the other hand, in many cases of human action done for a reason, even, e.g., when I go to that meeting only because I think I have a responsibility to do so, there is no explicit practical deliberation. And it hardly seems plausible that the underlying causal explanation of my action, if there is one, will always be radically different when I explicitly deliberate about whether to go, and in the end decide to go because I have a responsibility to do so, and when I don't deliberate at all but do go and go for just the same reason. So my suggestion is that if Dretske's theory is to be extended beyond the simplest cases of a single motive and the practical syllogism, two things are required: (1) the theory will need to be detached from psychological hedonism, and (2) principles of practical deliberation such as Goldman's principle L' will have to be examined in much greater detail. The first, one might think, involves at the least an expansion of the list of rewards suggested by Dretske as connected to pure desires. What is needed is a systematic way of making sense of anything that can sensibly be taken as a goal or purpose or pro attitude. Psychological hedonism may be true of some animals all of the time and is probably true of all animals some of the time. But many animals engage in apparently altruistic behavior that does not seem explainable by reference to Dretske's short list of rewards (for examples, see Dawkins 1976). And, of course, humans can have goals and purposes of an amazing variety and abstractness. So what is needed is a way of understanding Dretske's "pure desires" as one special case of ultimate goals or pro attitudes, correctly applicable only in some restricted circumstances. I won't pursue this problem here.

The second issue brings up both the problem of how to deal with conflicts of goals, such as the sort faced by the jackal in the simplest case, and the problem of how to deal with explicit practical reasoning. It is implausible to think that these problems are the same, since even animals that we probably want to say cannot engage in practical reasoning, such as jackals or for that matter rats, clearly experience conflicts of desires of the sort Dretske describes. And it may be that explicit practical deliberation brings in a range of goals and purposes, such as fulfilling a responsibility, not otherwise possible. In any case, the clearest examples we have of both these things, conflicts of motives and action on the basis of explicit beliefs and desires, are examples of explicit practical deliberation on the basis of which the agent then acts.

So even if in the end one wants to return to the project of trying to expand and generalize Dretske's causal account of the desire/belief model of behavior explanation in the ways I have suggested, it makes sense first to focus on Goldman's principle L' (and its analogues) considered merely as a principle of practical reasoning and independently of any connection with a causal analysis of desires and beliefs. This is what I will do in the next chapter.

5 Desires in the Explanation of Actions: Part 2, Intentional-Stance Explanations and Background Desires

In this chapter I want to look at some explanatory versions of the desire/belief model of an agent's reasons as expanded beyond what I called the "minimal" version explained in chapter 2 but that don't involve any obvious appeal to the supposed fact that desires (perhaps in conjunction with beliefs) are causes of actions, at least in any strong or problematic sense of "cause." In chapter 4 we looked at two versions of the desire/belief model of an agent's reasons that took seriously the idea that the explanations provided by this model are causal ones. We discovered that for both of these accounts much of the actual explanatory work is done by Goldman's principle L' (or some analogue), a principle that explains actions as issuing from a deliberative process in the agent and has nothing to do with causal laws or regularities. In this chapter we will look at accounts that explicitly invoke a principle of this sort but that do not claim that the resulting theory is a causal one. That is, the idea behind the accounts we will look at in this chapter is that we explain actions by putting ourselves in the agent's place, so to speak, and then trying to reason as he or she would or should. In Donald Davidson's words, "Reason-explanations make others intelligible to us only to the extent that we can recognize something like our own reasoning powers at work" (1987, 47). So in these accounts of the explanation of action, the explanatory force of the desires of the agent is supposed to come not from any alleged causal laws or regularities (or the like) involving desires but from the role that desires play in the practical reasoning of the agent whose action is being explained. The question here is to what extent desires, in any sense, really can be the elements of such reasoning.

DENNETT'S "INTENTIONAL STANCE" EXPLANATIONS

Perhaps the best-known version of this sort of account of the explanation of actions is the one given by Daniel Dennett. So Dennett's theory is an obvious place to start. Here is one way Dennett puts his idea of an "intentional stance" explanation of action[1] According to him,

We approach each other as *intentional systems,* that is, as entities whose behavior can be predicted by the method of attributing beliefs, desires, and rational acumen according to the following rough and ready principles:

(1) A system's beliefs are those it *ought to have,* given its perceptual capacities, its epistemic needs, and its biography. Thus, in general, its beliefs are both true and relevant to its life, and when false beliefs are attributed, special stories must be told to explain how the error resulted from the presence of features in the environment that are deceptive relative to the perceptual capacities of the system.

(2) A system's desires are those it *ought to have,* given its biological needs and the most practicable means of satisfying them. Thus intentional systems desire survival and procreation, and hence desire food, security, health, sex, wealth, power, influence, and so forth, and also whatever local ar-

rangements tend (in their eyes—given their beliefs) to further these ends in appropriate measure. Again, "abnormal" desires are attributable if special stories can be told.

(3) A system's behavior will consist of those acts that *it would be rational* for an agent with those beliefs and desires to perform. (Dennett 1987, 49)

Allowing for differences in terminology, this third principle of Dennett's can be most straightforwardly understood as being in essence Goldman's principle L', that is, as saying that from the agent's point of view, the rational thing to do is perform the action that would seem likely, so far as that agent can tell, to satisfy as many as possible of his or her desires. L', you will recall, is this: "If any agent S believes that hypothetical act-tree $A_1, A_2, \ldots,$ A_n (to be performed at t) is more likely, all in all, to achieve more of his desires than any other act-tree (that could be performed at t), and if S is in standard conditions with respect to each of his basic acts of this act-tree (at t), then S performs each of these basic acts (at t)" (Goldman 1970, 74). L' is thus more specific than (3) about the role of the agent's desires and beliefs in determining what it would be rational for him or her to do. Where (3) simply speaks of what "it would be rational" to do, given some desires and beliefs, L' specifies that the act to perform will be the one that, so far as the agent can tell, satisfies more of these desires than any other act open to him or her. (In spite of the differences in wording, I will assume to begin with that in fact Dennett means (3) to include the features made explicit in L'. We will examine below, especially in chapter 6, a different way of interpreting (3).)

With a bit of adjusting, therefore, Dennett's three points contain all the elements that I want to consider: roughly, that we can explain intentional actions by appeal to the rationality of the agent in performing them, given the beliefs and desires we have determined the agent to have. But *some* adjusting is needed, because there are really two distinct elements involved in intentional-stance explanations as Dennett describes them: first, there is a method of assigning desires and beliefs to agents, and second, there is a method for figuring out on the basis of these desires and beliefs what the agent will do. The first element involves what Dennett calls his "holistic logical behaviorism" (1987, 58) and is contained in (1) and (2) in the quotation above. But it is only the second element I want to discuss here, the element contained in (3) above.

Since I want to consider this form of explanation independently of any specific account of how we decide what desires and beliefs agents have, it makes sense just to drop Dennett's restriction, in the quotation above, to desires based on biological needs (and the connection of beliefs with perceptual capacities, etc.), as well as the specific list he gives. In fact, Dennett himself doesn't take this restriction or this specific list of desires very seriously. After all, animals, to which he thinks intentional-stance explanations apply, have few of the desires on his list (see Dennett 1987, 103–116, for an intentional-stance explanation applied to frogs). And one of his best-known examples of the application of this form of explanation, a chess-playing computer (Dennett 1971, 87–106), has none, since it has no biological needs at all. On the face of it, at least many, perhaps most, actions, and so many actions to which this form of explanation is intended to apply (e.g., my action of typing this particular sentence), are not explained by appeal to desires that are somehow based on biological needs, even at many steps removed, any more than they are explained by appeal to Dretske's "pure desires." So nothing is gained, and much could be lost, for the plausibility of this view by saddling it with such a contentious claim.

With these adjustments I am therefore setting aside or "bracketing off" the question of how we figure out what desires and beliefs the agent has. And in any case, on Dennett's account the reference to biological needs, perceptual capacities, and the like, was only needed to pin those down. I am setting aside as well the question of the ontological status of desires and the question of whether our ordinary talk of desires commits us to some form of realism about them.[2] This lets us focus on the central question of how we are supposed to figure out what the agent will do, according to Dennett, once we know, somehow or other, what his or her desires and beliefs are. The answer, it would appear, is that we simply put ourselves in the agent's shoes, so to speak, and then ask what it would be rational to do, given his or her beliefs and desires. This is how I understand (3) above, which says that any agent's "behavior will consist of those acts that *it would be rational* for an agent with [that agent's] beliefs and desires to perform." The question I want to ask is one that by this point must seem very familiar, namely whether "desires" here is intended to refer to what in chapter 1, I labeled "desires proper" or to what I call "pro attitudes"? As I will try to show, neither answer results in a view that is plausible, and hence a rather serious revision in (3) (or L') is needed.

If we take (3) as referring to desires proper, that is, desires in the sense in which it is possible to intentionally do something even though one has no desire whatever to do that thing, then using (3) to predict or explain behavior will result in numerous false predictions or fail completely to explain numerous actions. The example first considered in chapter 1 of my going to the meeting at my son's school will be one such case. In this case what I wanted to do was to stay home and read (i.e., in the proper-desire sense of "want"). What I actually did, however, was go to the meeting (because I believed that I had a responsibility to go). So with this sense of "desire," someone employing (3) to predict my behavior would have mistakenly predicted that I would stay home. And by the same token, someone trying to use (3) after the fact to explain my going to the meeting would have been totally at a loss for an explanation, since, by hypothesis, I had no *proper* desire to go. I went only because I thought I had a responsibility to go. So presumably this is not the sense of "desire" that Dennett intends to use in (3). (We will consider below an argument by Philip Pettit and Michael Smith that at least seems intended to defend the idea that desires proper can be used in this form of reasoning in accordance with Dennett's principle (3).) Thus we need to look at the other possibility, namely that the term "desire" as used in (3) refers to what I have labeled "pro attitudes."

This would be to understand (3) as saying, "A system's behavior will consist of those acts that *it would be rational* for an agent with those beliefs and [pro attitudes] to perform." As I have defined "pro attitude," it follows from the fact that a person intentionally performed an action that he or she had a pro attitude toward performing that action. This means, as I emphasized above, that *whatever* in fact moves a person to perform an action, including, e.g., a belief that he had a responsibility to do what he did, will count as a pro attitude. To put this another way, *anything* that could possibly move someone intentionally to perform some action will, ipso facto, be a possible pro attitude of the person toward performing the action.

This reading of (3) seems to be an improvement over the earlier one, which, after all, seems to come out false for many, or even most, ordinary cases. But this pro-attitude reading of (3) still presents us with a deep puzzle. The difficulty arises here when we ask how we are supposed to figure out what it is *rational* for some agent to do, given his or her beliefs and pro attitudes. To see this, consider a couple of further examples.

Suppose, to change Schiffer's earlier example somewhat, that I have an almost insatiable craving for chocolate, a craving that dominates my life. I spend virtually all my surplus money on chocolate, eat it whenever I can, spend much of my time figuring out how to acquire more of it, etc. No doubt if you know this about me, it will make predicting my actions rather easy. But are you predicting on the basis of what it is *rational* for me to do, given my beliefs and pro attitudes?

Or take another sort of case. Suppose that I have some admirable character trait, generosity, say. And I don't mean here that I make it a principle to be generous, by tithing or the like, as one might make it a principle always to tell the truth or to walk two miles every day. I just am in fact generous, in the way some saintly people, for instance, sometimes are: roughly speaking, my spontaneous acts are often acts of generosity, and when I deliberate before I act, it frequently occurs to me as an option that I can give something of mine to someone who can use it, and I give this option a fair amount of weight when deciding what to do. In this case as well, if you know this about me, you can better predict what I will do than if you don't. But the same question arises as before: are your predictions made on the basis of what it is rational for me to do, given my beliefs and pro attitudes?

If we try to understand (3) as saying that the agent will do what it is rational to do, given his or her beliefs and pro attitudes, then (3) doesn't seem to give the right sort of prediction in either of the two cases just considered, though for different reasons. If I have an overpowering craving for chocolate that virtually dominates my life, then surely the rational thing for me to do is to try somehow to gain control of it, perhaps by getting medical help. And if I am passing a candy store, have money in my pocket, etc., it is not at all obvious that it will be *rational* for me to buy and immediately eat the largest lump of chocolate I can afford, though given my craving, this might well be by far the most rational *prediction* someone who knows me could make as to what I will actually do. So in a case such as this, while there seems to be little problem in predicting what I will do, it is not at all clear that this prediction is based on what it would be rational for me to do, given my pro attitudes and beliefs. To think that it is would be to think that it is never rational to resist or override ones cravings or urges (or perhaps the strongest ones?), as if for some reason once one has such a craving, rationality requires that one act on it if possible.

Hume's dictum that "reason is and ought only to be the slave of the passions" might be understood as saying this, I suppose, i.e., that one not only will but should act on one's strongest cravings or urges, that is, that rationality requires doing so. But the question is why anyone should agree with this. There is a large difference between saying that this is in fact how people (frequently?) act and hence the safest ground for prediction (since one is the slave of one's cravings and urges) and saying that this is what rationality requires (i.e., that one ought to act on one's cravings and urges) even if one knows, e.g., that it will undermine one's health or ruin one's family. It is worth noting that what Hume actually says is, "Reason is, and ought only to be the slave of the passions, *and can never pretend to any other office than to serve and obey them*" (Hume 1964, bk. 2, pt. 3, sec. 3, p. 415; emphasis added). So it seems quite unlikely that he was speaking of cravings and urges, which at least sometimes do get successfully resisted.

A character trait such as generosity presents a different sort of problem. As Bernard Williams (1985, 10) has pointed out, one might have such a character trait without ever being aware of it. That is, a person who is in fact generous might never describe his or her options to himself or herself in such a way that the term "generosity," or any of its synonyms, comes into them at all. To others trying to predict such a person's actions, it might be clear that the best prediction in many cases is in favor of the generous act. But to the agent it might be that no thought of doing the generous thing or the like ever came into his or her practical deliberation. In fact, the same point could be made for almost any morally significant character trait, vicious ones perhaps even more plausibly than virtuous ones. It might help greatly in predicting someone's actions to know that he or she is stingy, cowardly, or dishonest, but it seems very unlikely that many stingy, cowardly, or dishonest people, when they are trying to decide what to do, describe the actions open to them using these terms.[3]

So the problem this presents for defenders of (3) is not so much whether it is rational to be generous or stingy (whatever exactly this might mean) but rather how one can maintain that a generous or stingy person has a pro attitude toward generous or stingy acts while the pro attitude serves as a basis for rational deliberation. That is, the intentional-stance method of explaining actions (or rather, the feature of it we are considering here) asks us to "get inside the agent's head," so to speak, and then, after we have figured out his or her beliefs and pro attitudes, decide on the basis of these what it would be rational for the agent to do. But a character trait such as generosity or stinginess, though it might be very important in explaining or predicting what someone will do, might not appear to the agent as a factor in deliberation *at all*.

I can put the point here in the form of a dilemma that the existence of such traits as generosity and stinginess presents for any defender of a pro-attitude reading of (3).

If we say that a generous person must have a pro attitude toward generous acts, since he or she intentionally performs acts that are indeed generous, even if not understood by the agent under this description, then we lose all force from the claim that we are basing our predictions on what it is rational to do from the agent's point of view, since, as I have just argued, such a person may not even conceive of these acts as acts of generosity, and so could hardly be using generosity as a factor in his or her rational deliberation. Alternatively, if we allow that since such an agent doesn't conceive of his or her acts as acts of generosity, we can't say that he or she has a pro attitude toward generous acts, then we are simply admitting that we are not basing our predictions of this agent's actions on what it would be *rational* for him or her to do, given his or her beliefs and pro attitudes. We are factoring in some weighting principles, such as a bias toward generous or stingy acts (or a disposition to perform such acts or to have the sorts of desires that would lead to performing them, etc.), which have nothing to do with rationality.

PRO ATTITUDES CANNOT BE ELEMENTS OF DELIBERATION

These sorts of counterexamples from cravings and character traits suggest that there is as much difficulty with (3) when we take it as referring to pro attitudes as when we understood it as referring to desires proper. But there is a deeper problem here, one that will let us see why (3) seems plausible only as long as we don't make the distinction between the two senses of "desire" urged in this book. Pro attitudes are just the wrong sorts of things to go into a principle like (3) as we are interpreting it, that is, into a principle about rationality from the agent's point of view.

If we distinguish between the point of view of the deliberating agent trying to figure out what to do and the point of view of someone trying to predict or (after the fact) explain the actions of the agent, then the pro attitude reading of (3) is extremely problematic. This is because there is just no way that a deliberating agent can *consider* his or her pro attitudes *as pro attitudes* in his or her rational deliberation about what to do.

If I am trying to figure out what to do in some situation, then I can discover only after the fact, so to speak, what my pro attitudes are and how strong they are. That is, I can only identify my own pro attitudes *after* I have done my best to figure out what factors are important and what unimportant, weighed these factors up as best I could, and finally acted on one (or some) of them. This is a logical point that depends on the meaning of the term "pro attitude." That I count a certain fact, say the fact that some action would be likely to secure for me a large amount of chocolate, very heavily in my deliberations about whether to perform this action shows that I have a pro attitude toward actions likely to secure me a large amount of chocolate. I may have various reasons (or none) for giving weight in my deliberations to the fact that some action is likely to secure me a large amount of chocolate. But whatever my reasons are, they cannot include my having a pro attitude toward acts likely to secure me large amounts of chocolate. This is not a *reason* for me to give weight to such acts; it *is* giving weight to such acts.

This is, in fact, much the same difficulty that, as we saw in chapter 2, arises for Williams's internal-reasons account of justifying reasons, i.e., that from the deliberating agent's point of view, his or her own pro attitudes are "invisible." In chapter 2, I argued that Williams's internal-reasons account of justifying reasons is empty, is indistinguishable from an external-reasons account, in essence because from the point of view of the deliberating agent no consideration on which he or she is considering acting (or to which he or she is considering giving weight in deliberating about what to do) could possibly fail to count as a pro attitude. That is, the internal-reasons claim that a necessary condition of some agent's having a justifying reason for performing some action is that he or she have a pro attitude to whose satisfaction this action would somehow contribute is a necessary condition that no agent could fail to meet by failing to have the pro attitude. Agents can make factual or logical mistakes about what will really contribute to satisfying some pro attitude. But it will never happen that they act on some consideration toward which they have no pro attitude. If they act on it, it follows that they had a pro attitude toward it.

This fact presents the same problem for intentional-stance explanations as it does for the internal-reasons account of justifying reasons. Just as it would do a deliberating agent no good for us to *advise* him or her to act on his or her pro attitudes, because there is no way of failing to so act, so it does us no good in *predicting or explaining* some agent's behavior to put ourselves in the agent's place and try to figure out what it would be rational to do, given some fixed set of pro attitudes (and factual beliefs). This would work only if all pro attitudes were proper desires that could be identified by the agent prior to deliberation, like a craving for peach ice cream. But though this will work for desires proper, in general the various other considerations bearing on action that any agent thinks of (or hears of or reads about, etc.) lack any feature that allows us to identify any of them as "one of my pro attitudes" *prior* to rational deliberation. Only after an agent has figured out as best as he or she can what is important and how important it is, that is, only after deliberation, can anyone, including the agent, see what his or her pro attitudes are. So it makes no sense to take pro attitudes as somehow the material of deliberation in a way that would be acceptable if we had only desires proper to consider. (We will return to this issue in chapter 6.)

One problem with trying to put pro attitudes into a principle like (3) comes out clearly if we consider a case where I have at least some motivated desires in Nagel's sense, such as the case described in chapter 1 when I decide to have another cup of coffee and so want to go into the kitchen, get the coffee off the shelf, and so on. Under the reading we are considering, (3) says that I will do what it would be rational for an agent with my beliefs and pro attitudes to do. That is, in the paradigm case at least, I first figure out what my beliefs and pro attitudes are (according to the analogues of Dennett's steps (1) and (2) above) and then figure out what it is rational to do, given these beliefs and pro attitudes. (And in those cases where there is no actual deliberation, what is rational is what a correctly carried-out process of deliberation *would* produce.) But this puts rationality into the process at the wrong point. I only *have* a motivated desire toward getting the coffee off the shelf, for instance, because I think this is necessary to carry out my decision to have another cup of coffee. That is, this desire, like many of the others in this case, only exists as a result of an *earlier* process of rational deliberation. They are, so to speak, the outputs of such a process, not, as (3) would have it, the inputs.

So it really makes sense only to talk about an agent's pro attitudes from a point of view outside whatever processes, rational or not, have led an agent to act intentionally. The considerations that an agent gives weight to and finally acts on *show* what that agent has pro attitudes toward. This will be the case whether these pro attitudes are the result of some sophisticated application to the facts at hand of an ethical theory about responsibility that I have been convinced of by reading moral philosophy, or are merely the result of some hormonal imbalance that produces an overwhelming craving for chocolate. Pro attitudes, in other words, though they may have different "strengths," in the sense of being more or less important as factors in explaining or predicting actions, do not, *as pro attitudes,* have different evaluative or rational importance. (This is one of the lessons of the chocolate example.) But then it is not clear that it makes any literal sense *at all* to speak of "what it would be rational for an agent with some set of beliefs and pro attitudes to do."

I am now in a position to put succinctly the problem with Dennett's (3). It is the by now familiar one that has affected many of the doctrines considered in this book, namely that (3) only seems plausible if we fail to distinguish pro attitudes from desires proper. It is only in the pro-attitude sense of "desire" that anyone who does something intentionally must have had a desire to do what he or she did. But if we understand (3) as speaking about actions it would be rational for an agent to perform, given his or her beliefs and pro attitudes, then (3) makes no literal sense. Predicting and explaining actions on the basis of an agent's pro attitudes are not based on what it is *rational* to do from anyone's point of view, either the agent's or the predictor's. These are matters of deciding what considerations move the agent and how much they do so. It only makes sense to speak of acts "it would be rational for an agent with [certain] beliefs and desires to perform" if we are speaking of desires proper, which can be rationally weighed and evaluated by a deliberating agent. But when (3) is read as referring to desires proper (an agent's "behavior will consist of those acts that it would be rational for an agent with [that agent's] beliefs and desires [proper] to perform"), what (3) asserts is just false. Agents in their deliberations very frequently (and rightly) give weight to, and act on, many other considerations than their desires proper. So (3) seems plausible, in the way in which we are interpreting it at least, only if we confuse pro attitudes with desires proper.

"BACKGROUND" AND "FOREGROUND" DESIRES

This same confusion, I think, explains the troubles that seem to be encountered by Philip Pettit and Michael Smith when they argue that though desires are always present in the "background" of an agent's decision to do something, they need not be present in the "foreground" of such a decision (Pettit and Smith 1990). Pettit and Smith give an account of how actions and decisions to act can be explained in terms of what I am calling desires proper. Or perhaps it would be fairer to say that this is *one natural way of taking* what they are claiming. I will try to show that their points are not valid if we understand them in this way but *are* valid if we understand them to be making and using the distinction between pro attitudes and desires proper. So it may well be that they do not intend their argument to be understood in the way in which it seems to me most natural to understand it.

In any case, in the context of the discussion of this chapter I will represent their account (I hope not unfairly) as an attempt to reply to my claim against Dennett that if we try to read intentional-stance explanations, and in particular principle (3) and other principles analogous to it, such as Goldman's principle L', as involving desires proper, then there will be many cases where false predictions or explanations are given.[4] Such falsity arises, I claimed, in any case where the pro attitude on which the agent acts is not a desire proper, such as when I go to a meeting because I believe I have a responsibility to do so.

Against this sort of point Pettit and Smith appear to argue that this does not show that desires proper are not always present when agents act, only that they are not always "present in the foreground." When this happens, they claim, a desire (proper) is still "present in the background."[5] Since, thus understood, their arguments, if correct, would both defend Dennett's principle (3) (and analogous principles such as L') and suggest that the distinction between pro attitudes and desires proper needed rethinking, it will be worth looking at what they say.

According to Pettit and Smith, "A desire is present in the background of an agent's decision if and only if it is part of the motivating reason for it: the rationalizing set of beliefs and desires which produce the decision. A desire is present in the foreground of the decision if and only if the agent believed he had that desire and was moved by the belief that a justifying reason for the decision was that the option chosen promised to satisfy that desire" (1990, 568). And the thesis they want to defend, which they call the strict background view, is that a desire is always present in the background of every decision to act. At the same time, however, they hold that it is not true that a desire is present in the foreground of every decision to act.

Unfortunately, the terminology Pettit and Smith use here is misleading (in fact, I think it misleads its authors themselves, as I will try to show below), and since, as I said, the points they are making are good ones *if correctly understood,* it will be worthwhile to sort this terminology out. In the first place, it is misleading to say that desires can be "present" in either the foreground or the background (or both), as if "present" meant the same thing in both these cases. It does not, as the quotation above shows. To say a desire is "present in the background" of an action or decision to act is to say that this desire partly *explains* the action or decision by being part of the agent's reason for acting in this way (it "rationalizes" the action, in the rather misleading terminology that Pettit and Smith follow Davidson in using). To say that a desire is "present in the foreground," however, is to say in part that an agent *believes* or *judges* that he or she has a certain desire. And on the face of it, at least, it would seem that believing that I have a desire is not a way of having the desire, not a way of the desire's being "present," anymore than believing that I have a million dollars is a way of having a million dollars (as Pettit and Smith seem to agree, since they give an example, which will be discussed below, in which someone falsely believes that he or she has some desire.)

Pettit and Smith compound the confusion here by adding to their explanation of a desire being "present in the foreground" of a decision that the agent "was moved [to act or decide to act] by the belief that a justifying reason for the decision was that the option chosen promised to satisfy the desire [that the agent believed he or she had]." So, according to their terminology, for a desire to be "present in the foreground" of a decision to act is

1. for the agent to believe (possibly falsely) that he or she has the desire,

2. for the agent to believe that the fact that the chosen action promised to satisfy this desire the agent believes he or she has is a "justifying reason" for so acting (or deciding so to act), and

3. for the agent to be moved to act or decide to act by this latter belief.

That is, it is neither the desire itself nor the belief mentioned in (1), the belief that the agent has this desire, that moves the agent in such a case. Rather, it is the belief mentioned in (2), the belief that the desire provides a justifying reason to act.

This is confusing enough that it misleads even Pettit and Smith, who, two sentences after the definition quoted above, give the following explanation of how a desire can be either "present in the background" without being "present in the foreground" or vice versa. "Suppose," they write, "that an agent wrongly believes that he has a certain desire D and that he should therefore ϕ; and suppose that he is moved to act by the desire, meta-D, to act in the way that would satisfy D, if he had it: that is, to ϕ. D figures here in the foreground but not in the background. And meta-D figures in the background but not, apparently, in the foreground" (1990, 568).

On their own account of when a desire is present in the foreground, however, this example is *not* one where D is present in the foreground. This is because, on their account of what it is for a desire to be present in the foreground, D will not be present in the foreground unless, besides believing that he or she has desire D, the agent believes that D provides a justifying reason for acting so as to satisfy it and the agent is moved to act *by this belief*. In their example, however, they specifically say that the agent is moved to act by yet *another* desire (which has conveniently appeared), called "meta-D," the desire to act in a way that would satisfy D if the agent had it. That is, in this example, though they say that the agent believes that he or she has a certain desire and believes that this justifies a certain action, what moves him or her to action is not this latter belief but yet another desire, meta-D, which apparently the agent can have without being aware of it.

Actually, it should not be surprising that Pettit and Smith get into this problem when trying to give an example, since unless they are equivocating on the term "desire" (which, therefore, they had better be), the theses they are arguing for are flatly inconsistent with their explanations of background and foreground desires. They claim, and illustrate (or rather, try to illustrate) with the example just discussed, that desires can be present in the foreground without being present in the background. According to them (to repeat), "A desire is present in the foreground of [a] decision if and only if the agent believed he had that desire and *was moved by the belief* that a justifying reason for the decision was that the option chosen promised to satisfy that desire" (emphasis added). But then if there really are, as Pettit and Smith say, cases where desires are present in the foreground, it follows that their main thesis is false. Their main thesis, which they call the "strict background view of desire," is, as I said, simply that a desire is always "present in the background" of every decision, i.e., that a desire is always part of the motivating reason for every decision. But in cases where desires are what they call present in the foreground, it is *not* any desire, it is a *belief* that he or she has a justifying reason of a certain sort, that moves the agent. So if there *are* any things of the sort Pettit and Smith call foreground desires (as they hold there are) then it follows that their main thesis, that a desire is always present in the background of every decision to act, is false.[6]

Denying that there actually are any foreground desires or dropping the offending clause (clause (3) in my paraphrase above) from the explanation of "present in the foreground" are only apparent solutions to this difficulty. Pettit and Smith seem clearly to want to hold, correctly I would say, that people sometimes act on *the basis of* deliberation. This means that something in deliberation (i.e., in the beliefs, judgments, and the like, that constitute deliberation) must move the agent to act. Taken as a whole, Pettit and Smith's explanation of desires "present in the foreground" is not a very plausible way of rendering this, even aside from the inconsistency in which it seems to involve them. This is because it only covers a small proportion of the desires (and other considerations) that the agent can consider in deliberation (i.e., that the agent believes he or she has, believes to be relevant, etc.) It doesn't cover all considerations that occur to the agent or that he or she thinks provide some reason to act, or even all the desires the agent thinks he or she has that he or she thinks provide some reason to act. It covers only those desires that (1) the agent thinks he or she has and (2) the agent thinks provide reason to act, when (3) the latter belief actually does move the agent to act. This seems much too limited, since deliberation can involve weighing things other than one's own desires, and of course other than only those desires that one believes constitute justifying reasons for acting. But the essential idea here, that people sometimes act on the basis of practical deliberation, seems correct.

If we stand back from the details of the account Pettit and Smith give, it is not difficult to see how to read their claims so as to make them true, though the reading I will give entails abandoning the idea that they have given a defense of the claim that the explanation of any action will refer essentially to a desire proper. On the one hand, in explaining intentional actions, we refer to desires and wants agents have. On the other hand, when agents act on the basis of deliberation, it is not their actual desires that they use in deliberation but their beliefs and judgments about these desires, along, of course, with beliefs and judgments about various other things. These two facts yield the "natural" distinction between background and foreground desires, whatever one may think about this choice of terminology, that is, the distinction between (a) the desires that we refer to in explaining or predicting actions, desires of which the agent may not even be aware, and (b) the desires the agent weighs up in the course of deliberation, that is, really, the desires referred to in the judgments or beliefs the agent has about his or her own desires (which is not to say that judgments or beliefs about other things too might not come into deliberation, of course).

If we use the terminology of this book and simply understand the desires referred to in (a) as pro attitudes and those referred to in (b) as desires proper, then Pettit and Smith's claims emerge as follows:

i. A pro attitude is involved in the explanation of every intentional action. (This is the analogue of the "strict background view" of desires.)

ii. Agents don't always consider in deliberation, or considering, don't always decide to act on, their desires proper. (This is the analogue of the claim that desires need not be "present in the foreground.")

Thus understood, both claims are true, though (i), since it is just a trivial consequence of the definition of "pro attitude," may be rather less than Pettit and Smith seem to have thought they were establishing. (Or perhaps it isn't, since most of the conclusions they draw in section 3 of their essay [1990, 578–591] are to the effect that adopting what they call "the strict background view" of the role of desire in the explanation of action is not sufficient to underwrite some of the more interesting, substantive conclusions that those who fail to make the background/foreground distinction have advocated.) It certainly doesn't show that a desire proper is always involved in the explanation of every action or decision to act. But by using my two different senses of "desire" instead of what they call "background desires" and "foreground desires," the suggestion in (i) and (ii) has the virtue of saving their views from inconsistency.

WHY IT IS EASY TO CONFLATE PRO ATTITUDES AND DESIRES PROPER

Failure to distinguish pro attitudes from desires proper, as we have seen, can lead to serious confusion. We saw in chapter 2 that it led to the thought that the internal-reasons account of justifying reasons somehow conflicts with an external-reasons view, and in chapter 3 that it helped to maintain the deeply implausible idea that all practical reasoning is or should be in the form of practical syllogisms. In this chapter I have tried to show that it can lend a completely spurious plausibility to principles such as Goldman's L' or Dennett's (3), or make such plausible (even trivial) claims as (i) and (ii) above seem to entail contradictions. It will be worthwhile, therefore, to try to figure out why a distinction so easily seen and so widely noticed still seems in practice so difficult to keep straight.

At least part of the explanation must be, of course, the fact that we use the same terms, "desire" and (especially) "want," to refer both to pro attitudes and desires proper. But I think there is a somewhat deeper explanation as well. My hypothesis is that the problem we have just seen to arise in Pettit and Smith's account of background and foreground desires is the real culprit or at least one of the main ones. That is, I suspect that much of the trouble is caused by attempting to combine, first, the obvious fact that people at least sometimes act *on the basis* of rational deliberation with, second, an account of desire that follows, e.g., Hume in seeing what I am calling desires proper as *the,* essentially causal, explanatory features in all action. Accepting this second point while failing to distinguish pro attitudes from desires proper leads naturally to the idea that desires are to be regarded as merely given, i.e., outside any deliberative or rational control, since if this were not the case, deliberation, and not desire, would provide the (or anyway an) essential explanatory feature of actions.

The combination of these two ideas then requires a model of rational deliberation that reconciles the fact of deliberation with the supposed central explanatory role of desires proper. This results in a model that positively invites us to fail to distinguish pro attitudes from desires proper. This model involves trying to understand rational deliberation as simply examining the desires we find ourselves with and then doing whatever it seems to us, given our beliefs, will be most likely to satisfy our strongest set of desires. That is, on this view, rational deliberation consists of, first, doing a kind of "vector analysis" of our desires, each of which will have both a strength and a "direction" (i.e., object or goal), and then, second, discounting for the probability, in our judgment, of being able to satisfy each desire by performing the various actions that we think are open to us. On this model, the rational act to perform (and for an observer to predict will be performed) will be the one that receives the highest score in this process. Desires here seem to provide all the causal or motivating force needed to explain actions, and as the things doing the causing, they are not themselves supposed to be subject to any sort of rational or deliberative adjustment. Deliberation simply consists of figuring out the direction in which the force that desires provide gets expressed.

This is, I suspect, the model implicitly behind Dennett's (3) and Goldman's L'. It is what makes these principles seem plausible. It is also the model that Williams appears to have in mind in at least some of his arguments for the internal-reasons view of justifying reasons. In reply, for instance, to the externalist suggestion that an agent might be moved to act by some consideration completely unconnected to his or her other motives, Williams says this shows why "it is very plausible to suppose that all external reason statements are false. For, *ex hypothesi,* there is [in such a situation] no motivation for the agent to deliberate *from,* to reach this new motivation" (Williams 1979, 8; emphasis in the original). Likewise, this is the model Pettit and Smith appear to be defending, though with some retrenchment. They notice that agents are not always aware of the desires they are supposed to be weighing up and acting on but claim that nevertheless these desires are still, like the convenient "meta-D," "present in the background."

Finally, this is, I claim, the model that is very nicely summed up by Goldman, as his views were explained in chapter 4. This model invites us to overlook the difference between pro attitudes and desires proper by, first, holding that we are automatically aware of our own desires (including their strength, presumably) and, second, holding that practical reasoning simply consists of reasoning in accordance with a principle such as Goldman's L' or Dennett's (3), which in essence simply tells us to figure out how best to satisfy the desires we have.

If clearly distinguishing pro attitudes from desires proper leads one to reject a vector-analysis model of desire/belief explanations of the kind Goldman suggests, the question that remains is what an acceptable model would look like. This is the question that I will address in chapter 6.

We can perhaps see the difference between Goldman's model and the deliberative one implicit in the argument I have been making in this book by contrasting both to a third, which I will call the "blind forces" model. On this model desires are simply blind forces that push and pull agents about rather in the way currents of air act on a falling leaf. Where the leaf eventually lands is determined by the (literally incalculable) interaction of the leaf with the molecules of gas in the air, dust particles, etc., that it encounters on its way to the ground (plus gravity, of course). Likewise, what the agent eventually does, according to the blind-forces model, is simply the outcome of the causal interaction of his or her desires with the "information states" in his or her brain. I don't think it is *too* much of a caricature to say that this is the model Fred Dretske aspires to. It is the one that would result if he could solve the multiple-desires problem, a simple version of which is exemplified by the jackal that has two pure desires that result in behavior different from what would be produced by either one by itself.

However, this blind-forces model is not Goldman's model, obviously, since Goldman allows, indeed requires, agents to be aware of their desires and, as I argued in chapter 4 this fact is crucial to the working of his model, since only if agents are aware of their desires can they apply principle L'. But the forces in Goldman's model are still *supposed to be* the same forces as in the blind-forces model (i.e., as Goldman wants us to understand them). Desires in Goldman's model are supposed to be causal forces, that is, forces whose role in the explanation of action is as causes, which are essentially unaffected by rational deliberation. In the previous two chapters I have offered several criticisms of the principle of reasoning this model employs (Goldman's L' or Dennett's (3)) based on the distinction between pro attitudes and desires proper. But, I am claiming, this model is constructed in such a way as to invite us to fail to make this distinction, primarily by characterizing desires *both* as causal forces essentially outside rational control *and* at the same time as elements of practical deliberation (because they are open to direct conscious awareness).

Desires, in other words, appear in Goldman's model as causal forces that we must simply accept but also are automatically aware of and hence (apparently) can use in practical reasoning. This is what lets Goldman move, in L', from characterizing practical deliberation as involving an agent's *beliefs* about his or her desires to saying, a few pages later, that practical inference is "where a person comes to have a certain want on the basis of some combination of other *wants* and beliefs" (1970, 100) and that "*wants* lead to basic acts via a series of practical inferences in which an agent's beliefs and perhaps additional *wants* come into play" (1970, 114; emphasis added). That is, Goldman shifts from describing practical reasoning, in L', as involving beliefs or judgments *about* desires, as, of course, it must if it is to be reasoning, to describing it as a sort of causal interaction between beliefs and desires themselves.

Goldman's model thus changes the blind-forces model by making the agent aware of the causal forces that are his or her desires. So on the face of it Goldman's model seems to make room for something like practical reasoning. But we can see that this doesn't really make sense, or at least doesn't make full sense, of practical deliberation if we consider a third model, what I will call (perhaps loading the terminology) the deliberative model. On this model, the agent weighs up the various considerations that seem to him or her to count for and against performing the various actions available and then performs that action that seems to have the most to recommend it, at least in the optimum case where there is no failure of rationality. The considerations here may include the likelihood of some act achieving some further goal or purpose, of course, but purposes are not restricted to the agent's desires proper. They can include whatever the agent thinks important, such as moral principles, religious doctrines, aesthetic theories, the desires of others, or whatever. Not only can these considerations include many other things beside the agent's desires proper; in contrast to Goldman's model, the amount by which the likelihood of success leads to discounting the worth of the action can vary with different considerations. Someone might think, for instance, that the barest possibility that an action would be dishonorable is enough to rule it out completely or, alternatively, that the fact that it is morally required means that it must be attempted, no matter how unlikely it is to succeed.

The deliberative model contrasts most sharply with the blind-forces model. The latter allows no genuine role for reasoning at all. There is simply a complex causal interaction among the agent's desires and beliefs that results in behavior. (So maybe, as Dretske at one point implies [1988, 121], we should be calling these states "desire analogues" and "belief analogues.") This is neither surprising nor objectionable, since the whole point of the blind-forces model is to give a causal analysis of the explanation of actions and hence, apparently, of at least some sequences of events that, on the deliberative model, get called practical reasoning. In contrast to the blind-forces model, the deliberative model allows for, and takes as a central notion, reasoning about purposes and goals, as well as about means to achieve them. And most important, it substitutes a completely different explanatory mechanism for the "causal forces" view of desire proposed by the blind-forces model. On the deliberative model, the reasoning process itself, together with the resulting decision, or formation of an intention, to perform some action, does the explanatory work, though what exactly this comes to has yet to be explained.

IMPULSE VERSUS DELIBERATION

Seen in this light, Goldman's model is an unhappy hybrid that tries unsuccessfully to combine elements of both the blind-forces model and the deliberative model. Indeed, it tries to combine two quite different explanatory mechanisms, "blind" causal interaction and conscious practical deliberation and choice. Yet another way of seeing why this is not plausible and, I hope, of at least making a start at seeing how to reconcile the blind-forces and deliberative models, is to notice that any account of desire/belief explanations will have to cover what are, intuitively at least, two very different sorts of cases: those in which I "think about what I am doing" and those in which I don't. This is a crucial distinction. To see clearly what it is, consider yet another version of the chocolate example. Suppose that as I walk through the kitchen, I am struck by a craving for some chocolate that I see in a jar on the counter and that I act on this craving by eating some of this chocolate. We can distinguish two cases.

The first case, which I will call the impulsive case, is this. I am walking through the kitchen thinking about, say, the nature of desire/belief explanations when I notice the candy jar full of chocolates on the counter. This awakens my craving for chocolate. Without ever breaking my train of thought I stop, open the jar, take out a couple of chocolates and start to eat them as I replace the lid on the jar and proceed on my way.

The second case I will call the deliberative case. We can imagine it to have happened on a different day, perhaps, or on the same day in a different possible world. Again I am walking through the kitchen thinking about desire/belief explanations, and again I notice the candy jar on the counter. Again this awakens my craving for chocolates. In this case, however, my train of thought is at least momentarily broken because I take my mother's advice to "think before you act." It occurs to me that there are some reasons for me not to eat any chocolates, reasons to weigh against my desire to eat some. For one thing, I have already had several chocolates today, and I believe that chocolates are both fattening and bad for the teeth. Then too other members of my family have been complaining that I eat a disproportionate share of the candy in our household and that I should leave more for them.

I decide, however, that none of these reasons is really all that telling when weighed against my craving for some chocolates. My teeth are fine, and I get enough exercise that gaining weight is not a problem. And since there are plenty of chocolates in the jar and I plan only to take a few, I will be leaving a lot for others. So I stop, open the jar, take out a couple of chocolates and start to eat them as I replace the lid on the jar, and proceed on my way. (Though I don't think anything turns on this, we can suppose, if we want to make these two cases as parallel as possible, that the only difference between them is "mental," i.e., that all my actual physical movements are the same in the deliberative case as in the impulsive case.)

In both these cases, I assume, the following three things are true:

THE ACT (A)   I intentionally opened the candy jar, took out some chocolates, and put them into my mouth.

THE DESIRE (D)   I wanted to eat some chocolates.[1]

THE BELIEF (B)   I believed that opening the candy jar, taking out some chocolates, and putting them into my mouth was a way of eating some chocolates.

The defenders of all three models of desire/belief explanations presumably must claim that in both of these cases, (D) and (B) explain (A).

To help us focus on the difference between the two cases and why this difference presents a different sort of problem to each of the three models, let us simply assume, as is plausible if we take (D) as describing a craving of mine, that in the impulsive case, (D) and (B) do indeed explain (A) unproblematically. We can then say that (B) and (D) together describe my reason for performing the action described in (A) (what Davidson [1980, 4] calls my "primary reason"). That is, in the impulsive case we are assuming that I intentionally opened the candy jar, took out some chocolates, and put them into my mouth *because* I wanted to eat some chocolates and believed that opening the candy jar, taking out some chocolates, and putting them into my mouth was a way of eating some chocolates.

On these assumptions, the deliberative case, however, seems problematic. The extra element present in the deliberative case but not the impulsive case is the small episode of practical deliberation in which I engaged before eating the chocolates. The problem this episode presents for the idea that in the deliberative case we can explain (A) simply by referring to (B) and (D) is that it also seems true that the action described by (A) was done *as a result of* my deliberation. If I had decided, say, that I really did have to pay more attention to my weight or that the other members of my household had a better claim on these chocolates than I, then I would have, or at least might have, decided not to perform the action described in (A).

So there are at least two difficulties with saying that in the deliberative case, as well as in the impulsive case, (B) and (D) explain (A). First, there is the question of how to understand the phrase "as a result of" in the claim that in the deliberative case I performed the action described in (A) as a result of my deliberation. I will return to this point in a moment. The second point is connected to the first one. It is that in the deliberative case it is not obvious that (D), *as we are reading it,* actually figures into the explanation of (A) at all.

My desire to eat some chocolates, which we are here supposing to take the form of a craving, comes into the deliberative case not as the factor that causes me to eat the chocolates, as it seems to in the impulsive case, but rather as something of which I take account in my deliberation about whether to eat the chocolates. That is, strictly speaking, when I deliberate about whether to perform the action described by (A), it is not the *fact* that I want to eat some chocolates but rather my *judgment* that I want to eat some chocolates that comes into the deliberation. My deliberation might proceed in exactly the same way even if my judgment that I wanted to eat some chocolates was simply mistaken (unlikely as it might be that one could make such a mistake).[2]

What this suggests is that in the deliberative case it is not (B) and (D) that explain (A) at all. My deliberation and the action I performed on the basis of it might have been exactly the same even if (D) had been false. It is rather (J), if anything, that does the explaining, along with (B):

THE JUDGMENT (J) I judge that I want to eat some chocolates.

But, of course, we can't simply say that in the deliberative case (J) and (B) explain (A). At the very least, this is much too simple, since it leaves out not only the other factors that I considered as possibly arguing against eating the chocolates (e.g., that they are fattening, etc.) but, much more important, it leaves out the fact that I regarded my desire to eat some chocolates as arguing in favor of my performing the action described in (A). I might well have judged that I had other, even much stronger desires but not thought that they were relevant to whether I should perform the action described in (A).

So an essential feature of my deliberation, and hence, one would think, an essential feature of any explanation of the action performed on the basis of this deliberation, is that I assigned the fact, as I judged it to be, that I wanted some chocolates a good deal of "weight" in my deliberation about whether to eat some chocolates. I will put (part of) this by saying that we need at the very least to add to our account of the deliberative case something like (R):

THE REASON-JUDGMENT (R) I regarded the fact that I wanted some chocolates as a reason for me to eat some chocolates.

More will certainly be needed in our explanation of the deliberative case than just (R), (J), and (B), since we will somehow have to record the fact that I also regarded my desire for some chocolates as arguing *more* strongly in favor of my eating some chocolates than the fact that they are fattening, etc., argued against eating them. And we will, of course, also need to add the fact that I judged the chocolates to be fattening, regarded this fact as arguing against my eating some, and so on.

But the important point here is that there is *apparently* no place for (D), as we are reading it, anywhere in the explanation of the deliberative case. The closest we get to (D) is (J), but, as I said, so far as (J) is concerned, (D) could be false. So the most straightforward conclusion to draw here would seem to be that if (B) and (D) together explain (A) in the impulsive case, they do not do so in the deliberative case.

Defenders of each of the three models of desire/belief explanation apparently take their models to apply to *both* cases and so will not want to accept that conclusion. I will explain in a moment (what is perhaps by this time already clear) how sliding into the pro-attitude sense of "desire" in (D) could lead one to think that. But it might be worth noticing in passing that there is a rather simple linguistic explanation of why this difference between these two sorts of case has been missed. In both these cases, if I am asked, after I perform the action described in (A), why I did what I did, the most truthful and straightforward answer will be, "I wanted to eat some chocolates." This will be true in the impulsive case because (D) explains my action and, of course, one is typically aware of one's own desires, especially when they are, as here, cravings. And this answer will be true in the deliberative case because (J) and (R) are true and formed the main basis for my action. Similarly, the phrase "the agent's reason" (that is, the use of "reason" labeled "(2)" in chapter 2 above) seems to apply indifferently to both my desire to eat some chocolates and my judgment *that* I have a desire to eat some chocolates, when either one of these explains my action. Thus in both the impulsive and the deliberative cases, it would be correct to say that my reason for performing the action described in (A) was that I wanted to eat some chocolates. In the light of this, then, it should be no surprise that the differences

between the impulsive and deliberative cases have sometimes been overlooked.

DIRECT AND REFLECTIVE DESIRE/BELIEF
EXPLANATIONS

Looking at ways in which one might try to resist the conclusion that (A) is not explained by (D) and (B) in the deliberative case will enable us to see once again why it is
important to distinguish pro attitudes from desires proper
and at the same time will help us sort out the three models
of desire/belief explanation that we have been considering
(that is, the blind-forces model, the vector-analysis model,
and the deliberative model). One view that I think we can
dismiss pretty much out of hand is that in the deliberative
case, (D) and (B) really do explain (A) in exactly the same
way we have been assuming that they do in the impulsive
case. If this were so, then, so far as I can see, it would
simply be false that I acted *on the basis of* my deliberation.
Neither (J), (R), nor my judgment that there were enough
chocolates left for the rest of my family, etc., would play
any role in the explanation of (A). Deliberation, on this
account, would be simply a kind of epiphenomenon, a set
of wheels that spun, or seemed to, but had no connection
to the mechanism by which the action described by (A) was
produced. The implausibility of such a position as a general account of the deliberative case seems to me simply to
rule it out from the start. (This is not to say, though, that
there are no cases where the agent at least apparently deliberates but where in fact his or her action is explained not
by this deliberation but by direct reference to one or more
of this agent's desires proper. Some cases of rationalization
might be like this. We will return to this issue below.)

A second, more plausible view would be to hold that (D) and (B) explain (A) in both the impulsive and deliberative cases but not so as to be incompatible with the claim that (J), (R), etc., explain (A) in the deliberative case. This sort of reply, though, will involve changing what exactly (D) means. The idea would be that since the action described by (A) is clearly intentional, there is a sense of "want" in which, even in the deliberative case, I must have wanted something I thought would be achieved by this action (in the limiting case, just to perform an action that fits the description). And since (J) and (R) (and perhaps the as yet unformulated "weighing principle" by which I proceeded in my deliberation) together describe what I am trying to achieve in performing the action described in (A), i.e., to satisfy what I judge to be my desire for some chocolates, the states of my mind described by (J), (R), etc., "count as a desire," so to speak, for purposes of the desire/belief model. That is, this second alternative would involve understanding "want" in (D) as what I have labeled a "pro attitude."

The thought behind this shift, in other words, would be that since the action described by (A) is intentional and since we want to hold to the thought that if an action is intentional then the agent must have believed that it was an act of a certain kind and wanted to or had a pro attitude toward performing an act of this kind, the only question in both the impulsive and deliberative cases is what this want or pro attitude actually was. In the impulsive case, the answer would be that it was my craving for some chocolates. And in the deliberative case, it was the combination of mental states described by (J), (R), etc.

This second reply, though it allows us to say that (D) and (B) explain (A) in both the impulsive and deliberative cases, obviously requires, as I said, that we change the way

182   we have been understanding (D). Originally, the deliberative case only seemed puzzling because it was placed in
contrast to the (apparently straightforward) impulsive
case. In the latter case it seemed that the desire and belief
described in (D) and (B) combined somehow to *cause* the
action described in (A). And the desire referred to in (D)
was, as I said, a craving, a desire proper. But whatever the
actual detailed mechanism of this causation, that is, whatever the mechanism by which this craving produces the action described in (A) in the impulsive case, the deliberative
case will have to be different. And this is because (J), (R),
etc. (the sentences by which we explain (A) in the deliberative case) can be true even if there is no such craving. And
in any case, no use is made of this craving in explaining (A)
in the deliberative case.

So if we now say, as this second reply would have us
say, that the judgments and other mental states described
in (J), (R), etc., are pro attitudes, that is, count as wants or
desires for purposes of desire/belief explanations, so as to
allow us to say that (D) and (B) explain (A) even in the
deliberative case, then it seems clear that the term "desire/
belief explanation" covers two quite different sorts of
cases. The mechanism, so to speak, by which (J), (R), etc.,
explain (A) in the deliberative case cannot be the same as
the one by which my craving for some chocolates explains
(A) in the impulsive case, since, by hypothesis, no such deliberation takes place in the impulsive case. And, as I have
said, (J), (R), etc., can explain (A) in the deliberative case
even if I have no craving for chocolates, that is, even if my
judgment described in (J) is false.

In short, then, this second reply changes the meaning
of "want" in (D) from a desire proper to a pro attitude. In
the sense with which we began the discussion of (D), a
craving for chocolates can be a want, but a judgment that
I have such a craving would not be. This is why the impul-

sive case, where (A) was explained by (B) and (D), seemed unproblematic, but the deliberative case, where (J), (R), etc., did the explaining, seemed mysterious. The second reply would have us say that in both cases, (B) and (D) explain (A) because "want" or "desire" can apply both to my craving for some chocolates and to my judgment that I have such a craving (plus my regarding this as a reason to eat chocolates, etc.). So the terms "want" and "desire" will cover two quite different sorts of cases.

An essential feature of the deliberative case, a feature so far not examined here at all, is that I decide or judge that my craving for some chocolates gives me more reason to perform the action described in (A) than the fact that they are fattening, etc., gives me not to perform this action. Had I decided differently, I would have, or at least might have, acted differently. But no such decision or judgment occurs in the impulsive case. This is another reason for thinking that in changing or extending the sense of "want" or "desire" from desires proper to pro attitudes, so that the same term covers both cases, we are allowing it to apply to situations where the actual, detailed explanation of the action are of two quite different forms, even if we end up saying that both are desire/belief explanations. To keep the two sorts of explanation distinct, I will call the sort in which the agent acts as he or she does as a result of some process of practical deliberation a "reflective desire/belief explanation." The other sort of explanation, where deliberation is not involved, that is, the sort that would apply to the impulsive case, I call a "direct desire/belief explanation." [3]

It is in large part, I suspect, failure to take seriously the difference between direct and reflective desire/belief explanations that causes many of the problems we have been looking at in this book by providing room for the thought that we need only one account of desire/belief explanations. So we are lead to accept a single account, such as the vector-analysis model of the sort Goldman gives, which tries to unite features of both direct and reflective desire/belief explanations. This failure to distinguish these two different sorts of desire/belief explanation parallels the failure to distinguish pro attitudes and desires proper. In fact, one might say that these two mistakes are in some way simply two sides of the same coin, since if the argument I have been making in the last few pages is correct, clearly distinguishing direct and reflective desire/belief explanations virtually forces us to distinguish desires proper from pro attitudes. On the other hand, if we focus on only one of these two sorts of desire/belief explanation, it is correspondingly easy to ignore one of the two senses of "desire." This is probably clearest for direct desire/belief explanations of the sort that seem to work for what I called the impulsive case of eating chocolate. The sort of explanation demanded by this case seems to require only the proper-desire sense of "desire," and so invites us to overlook the pro-attitude sense.

EVALUATING THE THREE MODELS

I suggest that the need for accounts of two different *sorts* of desire/belief explanations provides us with a way to evaluate clearly both the strengths and weaknesses of the three different models of desire/belief explanation we examined in the last two chapters. We have seen three quite different models of desire/belief explanations: (1) a blind-forces model, at least partly exemplified by Dretske's account, which sees desires (and beliefs) as blind causal forces and provides no obvious place for practical deliberation at all; (2) a vector-analysis model, exemplified by Goldman's account, which takes desires as causal forces that we are merely given but which allows for at least a form of practical deliberation about how to satisfy these desires; and (3) a deliberative model, implicit (I will argue below) in Dennett's account, which takes seriously the idea of acting on the basis of deliberation and which seems not to use a causal account of desire at all.

It seems clear that each of these three philosophers whose accounts we have examined takes his account as applying to *all* desire/belief explanations, that is, makes no distinction between direct and reflective desire/belief explanations. So, simply drawing this distinction goes a long way toward both sorting out the kind of trouble each account runs into and evaluating the prospects for patching up these accounts. If we restrict Dennett's intentional-stance account of desire/belief explanations to reflective desire/belief explanations, then, as I will try to explain below, though we will need to substitute another principle for Dennett's (3) (p. 149 above), we can avoid the sort of objection that comes from, e.g., the case of a person simply moved by a craving for something. This is the sort of case that needs to be explained by a direct desire/belief explanation rather than a reflective one.

Similarly, I suggest that Dretske's causal account of desire/belief explanations is much more plausible if understood as applying only to direct desire/belief explanations. This at least allows it to legitimately ignore the sorts of cases where it seems most implausible: those of conscious rational deliberation by adult humans. (We will return below to the issue of how, and indeed whether, this helps Dretske's account deal with conflicting desires of the sort exemplified by the jackal who wants both to run from the tiger and eat some of what the tiger has killed.)

The problems with what I have called the vector-analysis account of desire/belief explanations, on the other hand, the account exemplified nicely by Goldman's view, stand out sharply in light of the distinction between direct and reflective desire/belief explanations. This is because this view seems to involve, in an *essential* way, irreconcilable elements of each sort of desire/belief explanation. On the one side, like direct desire/belief explanations, this view regards desires as essentially causal forces, forces that provide the basic explanatory elements of action explanations. On the other side, like reflective desire/belief explanations, this view takes reasoning about desires (in accordance with L') as an essential feature of any action explanation. So it should come as no surprise that Goldman's view falls apart when we ask whether the desires it is speaking about are pro attitudes or desires proper. But if we overlook the distinction between pro attitudes and desires proper and at the same time do not notice the difference between direct and reflective desire/belief explanations, it will be easy to confuse the thought that since the agent acted intentionally, he or she wanted to do what was done, which is true as long as we are talking about pro attitudes, with the claim that it was a desire proper that caused or led the agent to act, which is frequently false.

There is an enormous difference between models of desire/belief explanation that, like Dennett's, depend for their explanatory force on some (normative) principle or principles of practical rationality, principles that purport to tell us how we ought to rationally weigh up our proper desires (perhaps along with other things), and models that, like Dretske's, involve no such principle of practical rationality but depend for their explanatory force on using desires and beliefs as causal forces that somehow combine to produce behavior. I have argued that each of the three accounts of desire/belief explanation we have examined suffers from a failure to distinguish pro attitudes from desires proper. My suggestion here is that once we see that there are two distinct sorts of desire/belief explanation, direct and reflective, we can see that while a vector-analysis account of the sort given by Goldman seems a hopeless attempt to conflate two quite different sorts of explanation, a blind-forces account of the sort proposed by Dretske and a deliberative account of the sort suggested by Dennett each look salvageable. We can understand them as applying to the two different sorts of desire/belief explanations, direct and reflective respectively.

So we are left, I suggest, with two sorts of desire/belief explanations, the direct and the reflective, for which accounts are needed and a proposed account for each, Dretske's and Dennett's. Since the main, obvious adjustment required for Dretske's account is simply to restrict it to direct desire/belief explanations, let us look briefly at some of the adjustments in Dennett's account needed to make it fully plausible as an account of reflective desire/belief explanations. We can then look briefly at the puzzling question of how one tells which of these two sorts of explanation is needed for any specific action.

It should be clear from above that Dennett's intentional-stance account of reflective desire/belief explanations, since it involves putting oneself into the agent's shoes and then figuring out what it would be rational for the agent to do, contains at its heart an unanalyzed notion of rational decision or choice. (This is an instance of what Dennett has sometimes referred to as "taking out intelligence loans" [Dennett 1971], that is, leaving a central intentionalistic notion temporarily unanalyzed in order to make progress on answering the question at hand.) That is perhaps the feature that most sharply distinguishes a model of reflective desire/belief explanations from one for direct desire/belief explanations of the sort Dretske suggests. I have no proposal for analyzing the notion of choice or decision in the intentional-stance account, but it is worth noting that eventually an analysis is needed that does not appeal to desires proper if reflective desire/belief explanations really are to be kept distinct from direct ones. By the same token (and not to beg the question as to where the burden of proof lies), advocates of some version of the blind-forces model, such as Dretske, unless they can provide an analysis of the notion of rational choice or decision in their own terms, will have to admit (what I am suggesting) that this model only applies to direct desire/belief explanations. As I argued in chapter 4, Dretske's difficulties with cases of multiple "pure" desires are only the tip of this particular iceberg.

There is another problem with Dennett's model, as so far explained, which, however can be corrected. Clearly Goldman's L', or Dennett's (3) as I have interpreted it, will not do as descriptions of the practical reasoning the deliberative model involves. These principles seem plausible only as long as we confuse pro attitudes with desires proper. But it should be possible to avoid this mistake and still give a description of the basic principle of practical rationality as envisioned by the deliberative model. Here is my suggestion:

PRINCIPLE OF PRACTICAL RATIONALITY Practical reasoning consists of a process that leads to deciding or intending to do what seems to the agent to be the best or most rational thing to do, in the circumstances, as he or she understands them.

This principle has several virtues when compared to Dennett's (3). It doesn't, of course, make the mistake about desires that it has been a main theme of this book to correct. Someone who simply weighs up his or her proper desires and then acts to satisfy the "strongest" set of them would be covered by this principle, since he or she would at least implicitly hold the view that this is the most rational way to act. But the principle would also cover someone who thinks that some or even all of his or her proper desires should be ignored in practical deliberation and who therefore acts on some completely different decision criteria, to use Goldman's term.

So a great advantage of this principle is that it doesn't make practical reasoning, and the resulting human action, appear more simple than it is. "Moral views, aesthetic principles, economic prejudices, social conventions, and public and private goals and values" (in Davidson's words [1980, 4]), not to mention political beliefs and religious convictions, all can and do play roles in practical deliberation. Knowing that a woman had been convinced by a particular Marxist argument about the justice of income redistribution, for instance, could be crucial in knowing why she raised her hand just when she did if, for example, she was voting at a public meeting on whether to support a specific tax proposal. So this principle has the consequence that the question of the rationality of the action at issue cannot be separated from the question of the rationality of holding any of the moral views, aesthetic principles, etc., that went into making it appear rational to the agent who performed it. That is, whether the Marxist's reasons for raising her hand were good reasons will depend crucially on whether the arguments for the justice of income redistribution that convinced her were themselves good ones.

By the same token, this principle leaves no room for the sort of quick and dirty moral skepticism that, as we saw in chapter 2, seems tempting if one ignores the distinction between pro attitudes and desires proper and so thinks of practical reasoning as necessarily a process of weighing up various kinds of desires. If skepticism about the rationality of acting on principles that don't connect to one's preexisting motives is to succeed, it will have to do so by earning its own way (like any other serious skepticism) by

showing that each alternative moral view, aesthetic principle, economic prejudice, social convention, etc., is for some
reason defective.

A connected point is this. The version of the deliberative model that uses the principle of practical rationality
allows for the fact that rationality is what Gallie (1955–
1956) has called an essentially contested concept, a fact
that, if not flatly incompatible with Goldman's L' or Dennett's (3), is at least problematic for anyone who accepts
these principles. (It is also a fact that the blind-forces
model, or at least Dretske's version of it, is nowhere near
being able to make sense of, which is another reason for
regarding this model as applying only to direct desire/belief
explanations.) If we think of practical reasoning, as Dennett's (3) or Goldman's L' would have us, as just a matter
of weighing up our proper desires and then figuring out
how to satisfy as many of them as possible, then, barring
factual disagreements or logical errors, it is hard to see how
there is any room for debate about the best thing to do.[4]
There might be several equally good things to do (that is,
all satisfy one's desires, or promise to, to the same extent)
but that is different. The principle of practical rationality,
however, allows for a fair-sized gap between understanding or predicting someone else's action and regarding his
or her action as rational. If one of us is a frothing-at-the-
mouth reactionary and the other is a wild-eyed socialist
and each knows the views of the other, then we may each
be able to predict and explain quite a range of the other's
behavior, including, for instance, voting behavior. And
each of us would be doing this on the basis of what we
knew seemed rational to the other in the circumstances, as
the principle of practical rationality suggests. But we could
do this while each held that the views, and hence actions,
of the other were deeply confused or mistaken in various
ways, and in that sense irrational. It may well be that such

sharp disagreements are only possible against a larger background of shared belief, as Davidson (1973–1974) has emphasized and Wittgenstein (1953, 88, par. 242) at least suggests. But putting oneself in the other person's shoes, in the way this version of the deliberative model requires, only involves seeing how the agent could have found the action desirable, not how one could find it desirable oneself. It involves seeing what Don Locke (1982, 246) calls the agent's "rationale" for the act, which doesn't necessarily mean holding it to be the rational thing to do in the circumstances.

THE NEED FOR TWO MODELS OF DESIRE/BELIEF EXPLANATION

Put in this way, we can see that the version of the deliberative model that takes the principle of practical rationality as the main principle requires two distinct features. One of these has been stated nicely by John McDowell. "When we explain an action in terms of the agent's reasons," he says, "we credit him with psychological states given which we can see how doing what he did, or attempted, would have appeared to him in some favorable light" (McDowell 1978, 14). That is, as Donald Davidson (1987, 47) writes, the contents of the agent's mental states must "entail that there is something desirable about the action, given the description under which the action is being explained." This "favorable light" condition gives a minimum condition for explaining an action by means of this model. We have to be able to see how the agent could have taken himself or herself as having a reason to act as he or she did. But this is not always enough by itself, and so another element is needed, since agents can take themselves to have reasons to do things, even good and sufficient reasons, and yet not do them. So the deliberative model also requires a notion of choice or decision or intention formation. As I have described the model so far, these notions are still simply unanalyzed elements crucial to the model. What counts as seeing some action in a favorable light, also remains unanalyzed here, of course. Someone who thinks that doing something would be enjoyable, say because he or she has what Schiffer calls an r-p desire to do it, such as a craving to have a cup of coffee, surely sees doing it in a favorable light. But though such examples are easily multiplied, this is not the same as saying what in particular, if anything, they have in common. Perhaps this is one place where the element of the deliberative model that involves putting oneself in the other person's place is essential. Perhaps, as Davidson and others have suggested, we simply can't understand as rational at all, and so can't apply the deliberative model of explanation to, anyone who seems to find desirable features of actions very much different from those we ourselves find desirable.

One advantage of holding that there are two different sorts of desire/belief explanation, direct and reflective, is that this seems to make more tractable problems that otherwise appear insoluble for accounts that (I claim) are best understood as applying only to one of these two sorts of explanation. Dretske's difficulties with multiple desires may be an example of this. If we regard his version of the blind-forces model as applying to all desire/belief explanations, then, as I suggested in chapter 4, the jackal with its two conflicting pure desires appears as simply the first in a very long series of increasingly more complex cases with which the model cannot deal. But if we know that somewhere in this series (perhaps even at this very first step?) we will in any case have to shift to the decidedly different deliberative model, this problem does not look insuperable.

Similarly for the "favorable light" feature of the deliberative model. If one holds that all desire/belief explanations are to be understood with some version of the deliberative model (as I think Dennett implicitly does for his version, for instance), then, even if we ignore my impulsive chocolate eating, how are we to understand those cases, mentioned by, e.g., Nagel (1986, 116), where each of two people has, and realizes he or she has, exactly the same reason to do something and yet one does it while the other does not? Such a case, assuming it is possible, would seem to require something other than the deliberative model to explain and hence seems to constitute something close to a counterexample to this model if we regard it as applying to all cases of desire/belief explanation. But if, as I am suggesting, we distinguish direct and reflective desire/belief explanations, cases of this sort will not appear as counterexamples. Instead, they will appear as especially puzzling instances of a more general problem, the problem of why one sort of explanation applies to some instances of intentional action and the other does not. They might turn out to be closely related to some cases of rationalization, for instance, where a reflective explanation that seems correct, even perhaps to the agent, in the end must give way to a direct explanation.

Consider the cases of two soldiers each of whom accepts the same moral or political arguments in favor of fighting the enemy and concludes that he should stand and fight, and each of whom feels (assuming this makes sense) the same amount of fear. But as it turns out, only one does stand and fight, while the other runs away out of fear. Here we seem to require a direct explanation, in terms of the agent's fear, to explain the cowardly act and a reflective explanation, which cites elements of the agent's practical deliberation, to explain the courageous one. Of course, this leaves us with the question of why one sort of explanation works for one soldier and the other for the other soldier. But the difficulty of this question should not deceive us into thinking that the possibility of situations of this sort somehow suggests that reflective explanations are not (sometimes) genuine explanations. This would happen, for instance, if one thought that because such situations are possible, even when a reflective explanation seems to work, we still need to appeal to a further desire that one agent has and the other does not (e.g., a desire to "follow reason" or the like).

But is this plausible? Even if we leave aside the problem that the only evidence for the existence of such a further desire is the fact that one agent acted on the basis of his deliberation and the other did not, i.e., the very fact to be explained, it is hard to see what the content of such a desire could possibly be. If we hold it to be a desire to follow the results of one's own deliberation, or the like, then appeal to such an alleged further desire is utterly vacuous. We still have the same question of why such a desire operates for some agents at some times and not for other agents or at other times. And if there were such a desire to follow the results of one's own deliberation, which an agent could have or lack at different times, then it would make sense to speak of the agent's reason for following the results of his or her own deliberation, and hence to ask whether this reason was a good reason. But this (I would say) makes no sense, any more than it makes sense to ask for my reason for believing the conclusions of my own best reasoning, as if even when I have cited all my reasons for believing something, there is always one more reason.

If, on the other hand, we restrict the content of this alleged further desire to fit the specific case in question (here, the two soldiers who act differently) and say that the one soldier simply has a proper desire to stand and fight, which the other does not have, then this sort of case loses all its general interest. Whether the one soldier has such a further desire and the other lacks it depends on the details of the specific case, which one would need to *know* rather than just make up. The claim that there must always be such a further specific desire, even when the agent apparently acts on the basis of his or her deliberation, receives little support from the discovery of some actual cases where there is, and none from merely citing a hypothetical one. What is of interest is the general claim (that the deliberative model never really works for reflective explanations without appeal to some further, deeper desire). If, as I am suggesting, there are really two different sorts of desire/belief explanations and these require two quite different explanatory models, then it should not be surprising that there are cases where it is hard to see exactly which model applies and why.

That leaves us, however, with a difficult question. I have been suggesting that the two salvageable models of action explanation are the ones I have been calling the blind-forces model and the revised version of the deliberative model and that these are plausible as accounts of direct and reflective desire/belief explanations respectively. Goldman's vector-analysis model is a hybrid that seems acceptable only if we fail to distinguish pro attitudes from desires proper and direct from reflective desire/belief explanations. A very plausible research project, represented in this book by Dretske's views, hopes to extend the blind-forces model to cover all cases of reasoning and intentional action, including the ones for which we use reflective explanations and that, I have argued, are amenable to explanation only by means of the deliberative model. The idea that human beings are just animals like any others, if greatly more complex, seems to give the blind-forces model imperialistic ambitions. Its advocates take it as applicable not merely to situations requiring direct desire/belief explanations but to all animal behavior, including the behavior of humans who have acted on the basis of deliberation. So my question is this: What if, though we are able to use the blind-forces model to explain animal and human behavior in cases that require direct desire/belief explanations, perhaps in something like the way Dretske suggests, we *never* get near using it to explain human action performed on the basis of rational deliberation, behavior that must be explained using the deliberative model? In short, what if, as I am suggesting, neither of these two models turns out to be plausibly eliminable in favor of the other? As J. L. Mackie (1991, 679) said of a different puzzle, "This is a very dark saying. *Why* should it be so?"

Notes

1 INTRODUCTION

1

Though sexual desires seem obviously connected to biology, it is not clear that people or other animals have a *need* for sex, strictly speaking. Perhaps "drive" or "urge" would be a better term here. Hence my reluctance to class sexual desire along with hunger and thirst. Since nothing below turns on this point, however, for simplicity I will continue to speak of all the desires in this set as having a corresponding biological need, while leaving it an open question whether sexual desire is really a member of this set.

2

John Searle (1983, 30) argues that we can see that "want" sentences must be taken as having sentential or propositional contents, rather than merely describing relations between persons and objects, by noticing that only on the former hypothesis can we understand a phrase such as "next summer" in a sentence like "I want your cabin next summer." Since this sentence can be used to report a *current* want, the phrase "next summer" clearly can't be modifying "want" here. So there must be a suppressed predicate (such as "to use" or "to rent") for "next summer" to modify. By itself, this doesn't tell us what exactly the logical form of such sentences is, but it does seem to rule out a straight-forward relational analysis, i.e., where desires are relations between persons and (intentional) objects, since any sentence of the form "*s* wants *x*" can take an adverbial modifier, such as "next summer," that, nevertheless, does not modify "wants." In what follows, I will assume that Searle is right in this conclusion and will follow standard, contemporary philosophic practice in regarding desires as proposition attitudes, without, however, assuming any particular account of propositional attitudes.

3

Galen Strawson, in lectures in 1992, argued that there is no impossibility in imagining a race of completely passive beings all of whose desires are of this sort.

4

Stephen Schiffer (1976) would deny that the propositional content is the same in these two cases, since he holds that thirst and at least some other "reason-providing desires" are self-referential in a way that desires generated by my decision to run in the race are not. But nothing hangs on this point here, and I will discuss Schiffer's views in some detail in chapter 3 below.

5

The connection between plans and intentions is discussed with great subtlety by Michael Bratman (1987).

6

The actual quotation is, "Who wills the end, wills (so far as reason has decisive influence on his actions) also the means which are indispensably necessary and in his power." Kant says in the very next sentence, "So far as willing is concerned, this proposition is analytic" (Kant 1947, 84–85, corresponding to p. 417 of the Prussian Academy Edition according to Paton). In fact, for "intend" at least, this doesn't seem analytic, since I might intend to have another cup of coffee without intending to get the coffee off the shelf, if, e.g., I did not believe it was on the shelf.

7

This second example also shows that Michael Smith is mistaken when he suggests that "an irreducible norm of practical reason" (when suitably qualified) is, "If A desires that he ϕs and he can ϕ by ψing then he desires that he ψs" (Smith 1987/1988, 246). Smith is not alone. Quite a number of other philosophers have accepted a similar principle; e.g., Alvin Goldman says that "if a man wants X and believes that Y is a means to X, then, characteristically, he will want Y" (1970, 99). But while I am still deliberating about whether to satisfy my desire for another cup of coffee, it is true that I want one but not that I want to get up and go into the kitchen to get one, even though I know perfectly well that this is the way to go about getting one.

8

This seems consistent with what Stephen Schiffer says about what he calls "reason-following desires," which, he says, are the same as Nagel's motivated desires (1976, 199, n. 4). Schiffer says, for instance, "Should one's desire to ϕ be an r-f-desire and should one in fact ϕ then there will be a reason which is both the reason for which one desires to ϕ and the reason for which one ϕs, and this reason will be entirely independent, logically, of the fact that one desires to ϕ" (Schiffer 1976, 197).

So far as I understand him, Schiffer's term "reason-following desires" covers both the sorts of cases I am claiming are covered by "motivated desires" as I use the term. Schiffer says, e.g., that "when one's desire is an r-f-desire one believes that even if one did not have the desire one would have reason to have it" (Schiffer 1976, 197).

9

It could be a form of this same mistake to say that my belief that I have a responsibility to go to the meeting "counts as a desire" for purposes of Nagel's entailment point, if by this is meant that the *thing* referred to as a "desire" turned out to be identical with this belief of mine. Nothing in Nagel's entailment point requires such a claim, nor indeed requires that the terms "desire" and "want" in this context refer to anything at all. So though I will sometimes say that my belief that I have a responsibility to go counts as a desire (or pro attitude) for the purposes of Nagel's entailment point, this and similar locutions should be taken as shorthand for something like (in this case) "I went because I believed I had a responsibility to go, and thus it follows that I wanted to do what I had a responsibility to do."

10

Davidson (1980, 4) gives a somewhat different explanation of pro attitudes than the one I give here but does not explicitly define this term in this essay. I think that there is evidence, however, that the use Davidson had in mind for the term "pro attitude" is at least close to the one I am trying to make explicit. He says, for instance, that pro attitudes include "desires, wantings, urges, promptings, and a great variety of moral *views,* aesthetic *principles,* economic *prejudices,* social *conventions,* and public and private *goals* and *values* in so far as these can be interpreted as attitudes of an agent directed toward actions of a certain kind" (1980, 4; emphasis added). This strongly implies that the term "pro attitude" is intended to cover much more than desires proper.

More recently Davidson has explained a pro attitude as "a disposition to act under specified conditions in specific ways" (1987, 41). This explanation, though vaguer, seems to have much the same force, though he may intend it differently, since he says this in the context of countering a suggestion he attributes to Philippa Foot and Thomas Nagel "that a belief alone is often adequate to spark off an action." According to my use of this term (and, I think, Davidson's original use), there is no conflict between the idea that a pro attitude is always involved in the

NOTES

explanation of intentional action and the idea that a belief alone might have led to an action, since at least some beliefs (e.g., moral views, aesthetic principles, economic prejudices, social conventions, etc.), if they move people to act, would count as pro attitudes.

11

I will consider Schiffer's claim that there are such things as reason-providing desires, as well as his characterization of the sorts of desires that deserve this label, below. See chapter 3.

12

The characterization of r-p desires given by Platts differs in some ways from the one given by Schiffer. For instance, as I understand him, Schiffer doesn't think it an essential feature of such desires that they have a specific phenomenological character, though Platts does.

13

Schiffer specifically gives thirst as an example of an r-p desire. So if my argument here is correct, either Schiffer and Platts disagree about how to characterize r-p desires or else Schiffer is not really entitled to this example. See my discussion of r-p desires in chapter 3 below.

2 DESIRES AS JUSTIFYING REASONS: INTERNAL REASONS

1

In announcing his goals for the essay, Davidson says that he will argue for two points in turn. The first of these is, "In order to understand how a reason of any kind rationalizes an action it is necessary and sufficient that we see, at least in essential outline, how to construct a primary reason" (Davidson 1980, 4). In the course of the argument, however, he says, "In order to turn the first 'and' to 'because' in 'He exercised *and* he wanted to reduce and thought exercise would do it' we must, as the basic move, augment condition C_1 with" condition C_2 (Davidson 1980, 11–12). And in a note to this sentence he adds, "I say 'as the basic move' to cancel the suggestion that C_1 and C_2 are jointly *sufficient* to define the relation of reasons to the actions they explain." In the original version of this essay he goes on to say in the same note, "I believe C_2 can be strengthened to make C_1 and C_2 sufficient as well as necessary conditions, but here I am concerned only with the claim that both are, as they stand, necessary" (Davidson 1963, 693). Later, however, even this belief that C_2 can be strengthened enough to make these two conditions sufficient for explanations of action is explicitly rejected by Davidson in the essay "Freedom to Act" (Davidson 1973), and the sentence expressing it is not reprinted with the rest of this essay in Davidson 1980.

2

Someone who holds that actions are identical with bodily movements will presumably also hold that these movements are explainable in straight physiological terms. Combining such a position with acceptance of the desire/belief model of action explanation would mean reading what I am calling the minimal version of the desire/belief model as saying that a necessary condition for explaining an action *as action* is that a primary reason like C_1 be given.

3

The terms "internal" and "external" have a rather confused history in recent philosophy, even if we focus only on questions of reasons and motives. Thomas Nagel (1970, 7), following Frankena (1958) and Falk (1948), uses these terms in connection with the question of whether it could be true that someone *morally ought* to perform some action without that person's being somehow moved to perform it. As Harry Silverstein (1983) makes clear, this is distinct from the question of whether someone could believe that he or she morally ought to do something without being moved to do it.

But the issue of whether motivation is or is not logically connected to, i.e., is or is not internal to, the truth of moral "ought" judgments or belief in such judgments is quite different from the broader question Williams addresses of whether or not motivation is internal to justifying reasons in general, since one can also have good reason to do what is in one's own interest, what brings one pleasure, and so on. And, of course, it makes a big difference what account is given of motivation and, in particular, whether or not motivation is connected to desires in some way, as Williams has them.

Someone who holds that moral beliefs all by themselves can move agents to actions without being connected to any additional item, such as a desire or other member of the agent's "subjective motivational set," would seem to count as an "assent internalist" in Silverstein's terminology but as an "external-reasons theorist" in Williams's terminology.

4

I think that Davidson in 1963 does pretty clearly intend his term "pro attitude" to mean essentially what I have defined this term to mean, though it may be that in 1987 he does not. See note 10, chapter 1.

NOTES

5

Dennis Stampe seems to hold that having a desire to do something is, at least sometimes, a sufficient condition for having a reason to do it, since he says, "The fact that I want something, in and of itself, is ordinarily a reason to act accordingly" (1987, 342). Williams himself, speaking of his internalist view of justifying reasons, says that he "actually think[s] that it provides a sufficient condition as well [as a necessary one]," though he only gives an argument for the claim that it provides a necessary condition (Williams 1989, 2).

6

For a discussion of what the internal-reasons theory looks like if we switch from pro attitudes to at least some sorts of desires proper as necessary conditions for having a good reason to act, see Schueler 1989.

7

Unless, perhaps, one wants to dig in one's heels here and claim that this version of internalism about justifying reasons is the sort of motivation-based moral skepticism mentioned in the Introduction. This would be to claim, e.g., that a person who has no desire proper to attend a meeting but believes it to be his responsibility to do so nevertheless has no (good) reason to do so. But pleasant as this result might be to those faced with such boring duties, this variety of internalism surely requires a strong, independent argument before it can be accepted. On this issue, see Korsgaard 1986.

8

Williams's own formulation of his internal-reasons view is more complex than this, as we have seen, since he wants to rule out cases where an agent has a motive but reasons badly about how to act on it. Hence he puts it by saying, "A has a reason to ϕ only if he could reach the conclusion to ϕ by a sound deliberative route from the motivations he already has" (Williams 1989, 2). Since I have already discussed this complexity, I am just going to set it aside for expository purposes in the discussion that follows.

9

Compare Davidson's remark that "The justifying role of a reason . . . depends upon the explanatory role, but the converse does not hold. Your stepping on my toes neither explains nor justifies my stepping on your toes unless I believe you stepped on my toes, but the belief alone, true or false, explains my action" (Davidson 1980, 8).

10

This seems to be what leads Philip Pettit and Michael Smith to invoke a desire they call "meta-D" to explain an agent's acting to satisfy a desire D that he falsely believes he has. "Meta-D," they say, is "the desire . . . to act in the way that would satisfy D, if he had it [i.e., D]" (Pettit and Smith 1990, 568). Their argument is discussed in chapter 5 below.

3   DESIRES AS JUSTIFYING REASONS: REASON-PROVIDING DESIRES AND THE PRACTICAL SYLLOGISM

1
See also Schueler 1989, 31–34. Audi (1989, 24–28) gives a good discussion of Aristotle's view of this issue.

4   DESIRES IN THE EXPLANATION OF ACTIONS: DESIRES AS CAUSES OF ACTION

1
Other philosophers, of course, have held that these descriptions (flipping the switch, turning on the light, etc.) describe one and the same act. An excellent recent summary of the issues surrounding this topic is given by Carl Ginet (1990, chap. 3), who offers a very sane adjudication of it as well.

2
Whether the rat can be imagined to be an *ethical* hedonist is problematic, though. This seems to depend on how reflective we imagine the rat to be. To use the practical syllogism, it would have to reason using only one premise specifying a goal or purpose. If it just as a matter of fact reasoned using only syllogisms that specified its own pleasure (or things that brought it pleasure, such as eating), then it would be a hedonist, all right, since it would be seeking only its own pleasure, but not necessarily an ethical hedonist, since ethical hedonism is a doctrine or principle about what is worth seeking. If we allow that it might at least *consider* other goals, such as finding out how the mechanism works or making the experimenter happy, then it would presumably also have to accept the principle that only its own pleasure (or only actions that brought it pleasurable things) is a reasonable or acceptable goal. This would make it an ethical hedonist, but it would also seem to undercut the idea that it was reasoning only in practical syllogisms. (Of course, it seems highly implausible to imagine that real rats, as opposed, say, to the cartoon variety, engage in genuine practical reasoning at all, let alone reasoning involving sophisticated evaluative principles.)

NOTES

5 DESIRES IN THE EXPLANATION OF ACTIONS: INTENTIONAL-STANCE EXPLANATIONS AND BACKGROUND DESIRES

1
See Dennett 1987 for variations on this type of explanation. The basic elements of this view have been defended by Dennett at least since Dennett 1971.

2
These latter are, of course, questions Dennett himself is very concerned with, since he holds, and much of his writing has been aimed toward arguing, that desires (and other mental states) as they appear in the folk-psychological explanations of ordinary language are "abstracta—calculation-bound entities or logical constructs" (Dennett 1987, 53). This contrasts with, e.g., Stephen Stich, who has argued for a realist account of our ordinary-language commitment in our talk of mental states. Stich's theory, stripped to essentials, says (e.g., for beliefs) that "when A says, 's believes that p', he is saying that s has a mental token of a sentence stored in the way characteristic of beliefs, and this token is content-identical to the one which he (A) expresses by uttering 'p' " (Stich 1983, 76).

3
There is an excellent discussion of explanations of actions that appeal to character traits (including the person's just being "no damned good") in Sturgeon 1985.

4
I don't mean, of course, that they had my actual claim in mind. Their paper predates this book by several years.

5
In the next few paragraphs, in discussing what Pettit and Smith say, I will try to stick to their terminology rather than mine is so far as this is possible. As will be seen, part of the problem, I claim, is that their terminology leads them into an inconsistency.

6
It is no good replying here that being moved by the belief is compatible with also being moved by some desire as well, as when my car is moved by the two of us if we both push it. Unless we are speaking of cases of overdeterminism, which do Pettit and Smith no good, since then the belief alone is enough to move me, "x moved one" is not compatible with "y moved one." If it is literally true that you moved the car, then, no matter how much grunting and groaning I was doing, it is not true that I did. (Of course, "You and I moved the car" entails neither "You moved

it" nor "I moved it," anymore than "Our votes elected the mayor" entails "My vote elected the mayor.")

6 TWO MODELS OF DESIRE/BELIEF EXPLANATION

1

Since the desire described here is a craving, it seems that we should understand it as a desire proper. As will become clear below, however, one of the issues raised by these two cases turns on whether we can intelligibly understand the desire described in (D) in this way in both cases.

2

It is easy to describe other, slightly more complex cases, however, where one can be mistaken about one's own desires (to say nothing of the psychologically deeper cases discussed, for instance, in psychotherapy). I might think that I want to see *The Big Sleep,* say, when in fact I have confused this with an entirely different movie, such as *Sleeper,* which is the one I really want to see. Since on virtually any analysis, desires have content, such mistakes are always in principle possible. In such a case it would at least be perfectly natural to say that my mistake was in my judgment about my desire, rather than in the desire itself. Clearly, there are lots of issues here that I am not addressing. (For instance, what distinguishes the case where I mistakenly judge I want to see *The Big Sleep* when what I really want is to see *Sleeper* from the case where I mistakenly want to see *The Big Sleep* when what I should want is to see *Sleeper?* These do seem to be different situations.)

3

Nothing turns on the terminology here. In particular, I don't think that direct desire/belief explanations apply only to "impulsive" cases, such as the example of eating chocolate.

4

This is reflected in Dennett's three principles (1987, 49), quoted at the beginning of chapter 5, and thus constitutes a reason for interpreting his principle (3), as I have, as being essentially similar to L'. Dennett allows for "abnormal" desires or beliefs, in principles (1) and (2), if "special stories" can be told. But there is not even that much room for disagreement in (3), which addresses what "it would be rational" to do, given the assigned desires and beliefs.

NOTES

References

Anscombe, G. E. M. 1963. *Intention,* 2nd ed. Ithaca: Cornell University Press.

Audi, Robert. 1973a. "Intending." *Journal of Philosophy* 70:387–403.

Audi, Robert. 1973b. "The Concept of Wanting." *Philosophical Studies* 24:1–21.

Audi, Robert. 1982. "A Theory of Practical Reasoning." *American Philosophical Quarterly* 19:25–39.

Audi, Robert. 1986. "Acting for Reasons." *Philosophical Review* 95:511–546.

Audi, Robert. 1989. *Practical Reasoning.* London: Routledge.

Audi, Robert. 1990. "An Internalist Conception of Rational Action." In Tomberlin 1990.

Aune, Bruce. 1977. *Reason and Action.* Dordrecht: D. Reidel Publishing Co.

Austin, J. L. 1970. "Intelligent Behaviour: A Critical Review of *The Concept of Mind.*" In *Ryle,* edited by Oscar P. Wood and George Pitcher. London: MacMillan.

Baier, Annette. 1985. "Actions, Passions, and Reasons." In her *Postures of the Mind.* Minneapolis: University of Minnesota Press.

Baker, Judith, and H. P. Grice. 1985. "Davidson on 'Weakness of the Will'." In Vermazen and Hintikka 1985.

Barnes, Gerald. 1977. "Some Remarks on Belief and Desire." *Philosophical Review* 86:340–349.

Beardsley, Monroe. 1978. "Intending." In *Values and Morals,*

208   edited by A. Goldman and J. Kim. Dordrecht: D. Reidel Publishing Co.

Beauchamp, Tom L., ed. 1974. *Philosophical Problems of Causation*. Encino: Dickenson Publishing Co.

Bennett, Jonathan. 1990. "Why Is Belief Involuntary?" *Analysis* 50:87–107.

Bennett, Jonathan. 1991. "Folk Psychological Explanations." In *The Future of Folk Psychology*, edited by John D. Greenwood. Cambridge: Cambridge University Press.

Bishop, John. 1989. *Natural Agency: An Essay on the Causal Theory of Action*. Cambridge: Cambridge University Press.

Bolton, Neil, ed. 1979. *Philosophical Problems in Psychology*. London: Methuen.

Bossi de Kirchner, Beatrig. 1989. "On the Power of Practical Reason." *Review of Metaphysics* 43:47–71.

Bradie, Michael, and Myles Brand, eds. 1980. *Action and Responsibility*. Bowling Green Studies in Applied Philosophy, no. 2. Bowling Green: Applied Philosophy Program.

Brand, Myles. 1984. *Intending and Acting*. Cambridge: MIT Press.

Brandt, Richard. 1989. "Practical Rationality: A Response." *Philosophy and Phenomenological Research* 50:125–130.

Brandt, Richard, and Jaegwon Kim. 1963. "Wants as Explanations of Actions." *Journal of Philosophy* 60:425–435.

Bratman, Michael E. 1987. *Intention, Plans, and Practical Reason*. Cambridge: Harvard University Press.

Brink, David. 1986. "Externalist Moral Realism." *Southern Journal of Philosophy* 24, suppl.: 23–41.

Campbell, Richmond. 1985. *Paradoxes of Rationality and Cooperation: Prisoner's Dilemma and Newcomb's Problem*. Vancouver: University of British Columbia Press.

Campbell, Richmond, and Lanning Sowden. 1984. "Sociobiology and the Possibility of Ethical Naturalism." In *Morality, Reason, and Truth*, edited by David Copp and David Zimmerman. Totowa: Rowman and Allanheld.

Carlson, George. 1985. "Hume and the Moral Realists." *Australasian Journal of Philosophy* 63:407–417.

Churchland, Paul M. 1989. "Folk Psychology and the Explanation of Human Action." In Tomberlin 1989.

209 Cohon, Rachel. 1986. "Are External Reasons Impossible?" *Ethics* 96:545–556.

Cohon, Rachel. 1988. "Hume and Humeanism in Ethics." *Pacific Philosophical Quarterly* 69:99–116.

Cummins, Robert. 1983. *The Nature of Psychological Explanation.* Cambridge: MIT Press.

Dahl, Norman O. 1984. *Practical Reason, Aristotle, and Weakness of Will.* Minneapolis: University of Minnesota Press.

Davidson, Donald. 1963. "Actions, Reasons, and Causes." *Journal of Philosophy* 60:685–700. Reprinted in Davidson 1980, to which page references are made except where noted.

Davidson, Donald. 1970. "How Is Weakness of the Will Possible?" In *Moral Concepts,* edited by Joel Feinberg. Oxford: Oxford University Press. Reprinted in Davidson 1980, to which page references are made.

Davidson, Donald. 1973. "Freedom to Act." In *Essays on Freedom of Action,* edited by T. Honderich. London: Routledge. Reprinted in Davidson 1980.

Davidson, Donald. 1973–1974. "On the Very Idea of a Conceptual Scheme." *Proceedings of the American Philosophical Association* 47:5–20.

Davidson, Donald. 1980. *Essays on Actions and Events.* Oxford: Oxford University Press.

Davidson, Donald. 1984. *Inquiries into Truth and Interpretation.* Oxford: Oxford University Press.

Davidson, Donald. 1987. "Problems in the Explanation of Action." In *Metaphysics and Morality,* edited by Philip Pettit, Richard Sylvan, and Jean Norman. Oxford: Blackwell.

Davis, Wayne. 1984. "A Causal Theory of Intending." *American Philosophical Quarterly* 21:43–54.

Dawkins, Richard. 1976. *The Selfish Gene.* Oxford: Oxford University Press.

Dennett, Daniel C. 1971. "Intentional Systems." *Journal of Philosophy* 68:87–106. Reprinted in Dennett 1978.

Dennett, Daniel C. 1978. *Brainstorms.* Montgomery, Vt.: Bradford Books.

Dennett, Daniel C. 1987. *The Intentional Stance.* Cambridge: MIT Press.

Dennett, Daniel C. 1991. "Real Patterns." *Journal of Philosophy* 88:27–51.

Dent, N. J. H. 1985. *The Moral Psychology of the Virtues.* Cambridge: Cambridge University Press.

De Sousa, Ronald. 1987. *The Rationality of Emotion.* Cambridge: MIT Press.

Donagan, Alan. 1987. *Choice: The Essential Element in Human Action.* London: Routledge.

Dretske, Fred. 1988. *Explaining Behavior: Reasons in a World of Causes.* Cambridge: MIT Press.

Dretske, Fred. 1989. "Reasons and Causes." In Tomberlin 1989.

Dunn, Robert. 1987. *Weakness of Will.* Indianapolis: Hackett.

Evnine, Simon. 1991. *Donald Davidson.* Stanford: Stanford University Press.

Falk, W. D. 1948. " 'Ought' and Motivation." *Aristotelian Society Proceedings* 48:111–138. Reprinted in Falk 1986.

Falk, W. D. 1963. "Action Guiding Reasons." *Journal of Philosophy* 60:702–718. Reprinted in Falk 1986.

Falk, W. D. 1975. "Hume on Practical Reason." *Philosophical Studies* 27:1–18. Reprinted in Falk 1986.

Falk, W. D. 1986. *Ought, Reasons, and Morality.* Ithaca: Cornell University Press.

Feinberg, Joel. 1970. "Causing Voluntary Actions." In his *Doing and Deserving.* Princeton: Princeton University Press.

Fisher, John Martin, ed. 1986. *Moral Responsibility.* Ithaca: Cornell University Press.

Føllesdal, Dagfinn. 1985. "Causation and Explanation: A Problem in Davidson's View on Action and Mind." In LaPore and McLaughlin 1985.

Foot, Philippa. 1978. *Virtues and Vices.* Oxford: Oxford University Press.

Frankena, W. K. 1958. "Obligation and Motivation in Recent Moral Philosophy." In *Essays in Moral Philosophy,* edited by A. I. Melden. Seattle: University of Washington Press.

Gallie, W. B. 1955–1956. "Essentially Contested Concepts." *Aristotelian Society Proceedings* 56:167–198.

Gauthier, David. 1963. *Practical Reasoning.* Oxford: Oxford University Press.

Ginet, Carl. 1989. "Reasons in Explanation of Action: An Incompatibilist Account." In Tomberlin 1989.

REFERENCES

Ginet, Carl. 1990. *On Action*. Cambridge: Cambridge University Press.

Goldman, Alvin. 1970. *A Theory of Human Action*. Princeton: Princeton University Press.

Gosling, Justin. 1969. *Pleasure and Desire*. Oxford: Clarendon Press.

Gosling, Justin. 1990. *Weakness of the Will*. London: Routledge.

Grandy, R., and R. Warner, eds. 1986. *Philosophical Grounds of Rationality*. Oxford: Oxford University Press.

Greenwood, John D., ed. 1991. *The Future of Folk Psychology*. Cambridge: Cambridge University Press.

Grice, G. R. 1978. "Are There Reasons for Acting?" In *Studies in Ethical Theory*, edited by Peter A. French, Theodore E. Uehling, Jr., and Howard K. Wettstein, Midwest Studies in Philosophy, no. 3. Minneapolis: University of Minnesota Press.

Grice, H. P. 1957. "Meaning." *Philosophical Review* 66:377–388. Reprinted in Grice 1989.

Grice, H. P. 1971. "Intention and Uncertainty." *Proceedings of the British Academy* 57:263–279.

Grice, H. P. 1989. *Studies in the Way of Words*. Cambridge: Harvard University Press.

Grice, H. P. 1991. *The Conception of Value*. Oxford: Oxford University Press.

Grice, H. P., and Judith Baker. 1985. "Davidson on 'Weakness of the Will'." In Vermazen and Hintikka 1985.

Gustafson, Donald F. 1973. "A Critical Survey of the Reasons vs. Causes Argument in Recent Philosophy of Action." *Metaphilosophy* 4:269–297.

Gustafson, Donald F. 1986a. "Agency and Psychological Causation." In Gustafson 1986b.

Gustafson, Donald F. 1986b. *Intention and Agency*. Dordrecht: D. Reidel Publishing Co.

Hamlyn, D. W. 1964. "Causality and Human Behaviour." *Aristotelian Society Proceedings*, suppl. vol. 38: 125–142.

Harman, Gilbert. 1976. "Practical Reasoning." *Review of Metaphysics* 29:431–463.

Harman, Gilbert. 1986a. *Change in View*. Cambridge: MIT Press.

212   Harman, Gilbert. 1986b. "Willing and Intending." In Grandy and Warner 1986.

Hart, W. D. 1988. *The Engines of the Soul.* Cambridge: Cambridge University Press.

Heil, John. 1981. "Does Cognitive Psychology Rest on a Mistake?" *Mind* 90:321–342.

Hill, Thomas. 1989. "Kant's Theory of Practical Reason." *Monist* 72:363–383.

Honderich, Ted. 1988. *A Theory of Determinism.* Oxford: Oxford University Press.

Horgan, Terence. 1989. "Mental Quasation." In Tomberlin 1989.

Horgan, Terence, and James Woodward. 1985. "Folk Psychology Is Here to Stay." *Philosophical Review* 94:197–226.

Hornsby, Jennifer. 1980. *Actions.* London: Routledge and Kegan Paul.

Hume, David. 1964. *A Treatise of Human Nature.* Edited by L. A. Selby-Bigge. Oxford: Oxford University Press. First published in 1739.

Hurley, Paul. 1989. "Where the Traditional Accounts of Practical Reason Go Wrong." *Logos* 10:157–166.

Hurley, S. L. 1989. *Natural Reasons.* Oxford: Oxford University Press.

Hursthouse, Rosalind. 1991. "Arational Actions." *Journal of Philosophy* 88:57–68.

Kant, I. 1947. *Groundwork of the Metaphysic of Morals.* Translated by H. J. Paton. London: Hutchinson's University Library. First published in 1785.

Kenny, Anthony. 1989. *The Metaphysics of Mind.* Oxford: Oxford University Press.

Kim, Jaegwon. 1984. "Epiphenomenal and Supervenient Causation." In *Causation and Causal Theories,* edited by Peter A. French, Theodore E. Uehling, Jr., and Howard K. Wettstein, Midwest Studies in Philosophy, no. 9. Minneapolis: University of Minnesota Press.

Kim, Jaegwon. 1987. "Explanatory Realism, Causal Realism, and Explanatory Exclusion." In *Realism and Antirealism,* edited by Peter A. French, Theodore E. Uehling, Jr., and Howard K. Wettstein, Midwest Studies in Philosophy, no. 12. Minneapolis: University of Minnesota Press.

213   Kim, Jaegwon, and Richard Brandt. 1963. "Wants as Explanations of Actions." *Journal of Philosophy* 60:425–435.

Korsgaard, Christine. 1986. "Skepticism about Practical Reason." *Journal of Philosophy* 83:5–25.

LaPore, Ernest, and Brian P. McLaughlin, eds. 1985. *Actions and Events: Perspectives on the Philosophy of Donald Davidson*. Oxford: Blackwell.

Lehrer, Keith. 1989. "Metamental Ascent: Beyond Belief and Desire." *Proceedings and Addresses of the American Philosophical Association* 63, no. 3: 19–30.

Lennon, Kathleen. 1990. *Explaining Human Action*. London: Duckworth.

Lewis, David. 1988. "Desire as Belief." *Mind* 97:323–332.

Locke, Don. 1982. "Beliefs, Desires, and Reasons for Action." *American Philosophical Quarterly* 19:241–249.

Lycan, William G. 1987. *Consciousness*. Cambridge: MIT Press.

MacDonald, Scott. 1991. "Ultimate Ends in Practical Reasoning." *Philosophical Review,* Jan.

Mackie, J. L. 1979. "Mind, Brain, and Causation." In *Studies in Metaphysics,* edited by Peter A. French, Theodore E. Uehling, Jr., and Howard K. Wettstein, Midwest Studies in Philosophy, no. 4. Minneapolis: University of Minnesota Press.

Mackie, J. L. 1980. *Hume's Moral Theory*. London: Routledge and Kegan Paul.

Mackie, J. L. 1991. "Retributivism: A Test Case for Ethical Objectivity." In *Philosophy of Law,* 4th ed., edited by Joel Feinberg and Hyman Gross. Belmont: Wadsworth.

Marks, Joel, ed. 1986. *Ways of Desire*. Chicago: Precedent Publishing.

McDowell, John. 1978. "Are Moral Requirements Hypothetical Imperatives?" *Aristotelian Society Proceedings,* suppl. vol. 52: 13–29.

McDowell, John. 1979. "Virtue and Reason." *Monist* 6:333–350.

McDowell, John. 1982. "Reason and Action." *Philosophical Investigations* 5:301–305.

McGinn, C. 1979. "Action and Its Explanation." In *Philosophical Problems in Psychology,* edited by N. Bolton. London: Methuen.

214   McLaughlin, Brian P., and Ernest LaPore, eds. 1985. *Actions and Events: Perspectives on the Philosophy of Donald Davidson.* Oxford: Blackwell.

Meiland, Jack. 1970. *The Nature of Intention.* London: Methuen.

Mele, Alfred. 1987. *Irrationality.* Oxford: Oxford University Press.

Mele, Alfred. 1989. "Motivational Internalism: The Powers and Limits of Practical Reasoning." *Philosophia* (Israel) 19:417–436.

Milo, Ronald D. 1984. "Moral Weakness." In his *Immorality.* Princeton: Princeton University Press.

Nagel, Thomas. 1970. *The Possibility of Altruism.* Oxford: Oxford University Press.

Nagel, Thomas. 1986. *The View from Nowhere.* Oxford: Oxford University Press.

O'Neill, Onora. 1975. *Acting on Principle.* New York: Columbia University Press.

O'Neill, Onora. 1989. "Reason and Autonomy in *Grundlegung* III." In her *Constructions of Reason.* Cambridge: Cambridge University Press.

O'Shaughnessy, Brian. 1973. "Trying (as the Mental 'Pineal Gland')." *Journal of Philosophy* 70:365–386.

O'Shaughnessy, Brian. 1980. *The Will.* Cambridge: Cambridge University Press.

Parfit, Derek. 1984. *Reasons and Persons.* Oxford: Oxford University Press.

Pears, David. 1975. "Sketch for a Causal Theory of Wanting and Doing." In his *Questions in the Philosophy of Mind.* London: Duckworth.

Pears, David. 1984. *Motivated Irrationality.* Oxford: Oxford University Press.

Pettit, Philip. 1987. "Humeans, Anti-Humeans, and Motivation." *Mind* 96:530–533.

Pettit, Philip, and Michael Smith. 1990. "Backgrounding Desire." *Philosophical Review* 99:565–592.

Platts, Mark. 1991. *Moral Realities.* London: Routledge.

Postow, B. C. 1989. "Criteria for Theories of Practical Rationality." *Philosophy and Phemenological Research* 50:69–87.

Putnam, H. 1982. "The Transcendence of Reason." *Synthese* 51:141–167

Putnam, H. 1983. "Why Reason Can't Be Naturalized." *Synthese* 52:3–23.

Raz, Joseph. 1975. *Practical Reason and Norms.* London: Hutchison.

Raz, Joseph, ed. 1978. *Practical Reasoning.* Oxford: Oxford University Press.

Raz, Joseph. 1986. *The Morality of Freedom.* Oxford: Oxford University Press.

Richards, David A. J. 1970. *A Theory of Reasons for Action.* Oxford: Oxford University Press.

Rorty, Amélie Oksenberg, ed. 1980a. *Essays on Aristotle's Ethics.* Berkeley: University of California Press.

Rorty, Amélie Oksenberg, ed. 1980b. *Explaining Emotions.* Berkeley: University of California Press.

Rosenberg, Alexander. 1980. *Sociobiology and the Preemption of Social Science.* Baltimore: Johns Hopkins University Press.

Rosenberg, Alexander. 1988. *Philosophy of Social Science.* Boulder: Westview Press.

Ryle, Gilbert. 1949. *The Concept of Mind.* New York: Barnes and Noble.

Sayre-McCord, Geoffrey, ed. 1988. *Essays on Moral Realism.* Ithaca: Cornell University Press.

Sayre-McCord, Geoffrey. 1989. "Functional Explanations and Reasons as Causes." In Tomberlin 1989.

Scanlon, T. M. 1975. "Preference and Urgency." *Journal of Philosophy* 72:655–669.

Scheffler, Samuel. 1982. *The Rejection of Consequentialism.* Oxford: Oxford University Press.

Schiffer, Stephen. 1976. "A Paradox of Desire." *American Philosophical Quarterly* 13:195–203.

Schueler, G. F. 1979. "Exclusionary Reasons." *Personalist* 60:407–410.

Schueler, G. F. 1983. "Akrasia Revisited." *Mind* 92:580–584.

Schueler, G. F. 1984. "Some Reasoning about Preferences." *Ethics* 95:78–80.

216   Schueler, G. F. 1988. "Modus Ponens and Moral Realism." *Ethics* 98:492–500.

Schueler, G. F. 1989. *The Idea of a Reason for Acting.* Lewiston: Edwin Mellen.

Schueler, G. F. 1991a. "Anti-realism and Skepticism in Ethics." *Iyyun: The Jerusalem Philosophical Quarterly* 4:3–18.

Schueler, G. F. 1991b. "Pro-attitudes and Direction of Fit." *Mind* 100:277–281.

Searle, John R. 1983. *Intentionality.* Cambridge: Cambridge University Press.

Silverstein, Harry S. 1983. "Assenting to 'Ought' Judgments." *Noûs* 17:159–182.

Slote, Michael. 1983. "Goods and Reasons." In his *Goods and Virtues.* Oxford: Oxford University Press.

Smith, Michael. 1987. "The Humean Theory of Motivation." *Mind* 96:36–61.

Smith, Michael. 1987–1988. "Reason and Desire." *Aristotelian Society Proceedings* 88:246–247.

Smith, Michael, and Philip Pettit. 1990. "Backgrounding Desire." *Philosophical Review* 99:565–592.

Solomon, Robert C. 1980. "Emotion and Choice." In Rorty 1980b.

Sowden, Lanning, and Richmond Campbell. 1984. "Sociobiology and the Possibility of Ethical Naturalism." In *Morality, Reason, and Truth,* edited by David Copp and David Zimmerman. Totowa: Rowman and Allanheld.

Stampe, Dennis W. 1987. "The Authority of Desire." *Philosophical Review* 96:341–381.

Stich, Stephen. 1983. *From Folk Psychology to Cognitive Science.* Cambridge: MIT Press.

Stocker, Michael. 1980. "Intellectual Desire, Emotion, and Action." In Rorty 1980b.

Sturgeon, Nicholas L. 1985. "Moral Explanations." In *Morality, Reason, and Truth,* edited by David Copp and David Zimmerman. Totowa: Rowman and Allanheld.

Taylor, Charles. 1964. *The Explanation of Behaviour.* London: Routledge and Kegan Paul.

Taylor, Charles. 1981. "Understanding and Explanation in the

217   *Geisteswissenschaften.*" In *Wittgenstein: To Follow a Rule,* edited by Steven H. Holtzman and Christopher M. Leich. London: Routledge and Kegan Paul.

Taylor, Charles. 1982. "Rationality." In *Rationality and Relativism,* edited by Martin Hollis and Steven Lukes. Oxford: Blackwell.

Taylor, Gabriele. 1985. *Pride, Shame, and Guilt: Emotions of Self-Assessment.* Oxford: Oxford University Press.

Thomson, Judith Jarvis. 1977. *Acts and Other Events.* Ithaca: Cornell University Press.

Tomberlin, James E., ed. 1989. *Philosophy of Mind and Action Theory, 1989.* Philosophical Perspectives, no. 3. Atascadero: Ridgeview Publishing Co.

Tomberlin, James E., ed. 1990. *Action Theory and Philosophy of Mind, 1990.* Philosophical Perspectives, no. 4. Atascadero: Ridgeview Publishing Co.

Velleman, David J. 1985. "Practical Reflection." *Philosophical Review* 94:33–61.

Velleman, David J. 1989. *Practical Reflection.* Princeton: Princeton University Press.

Vermazen, Bruce. 1980. "Occurrent and Standing Wants." In *Action and Responsibility,* edited by Michael Bradie and Myles Brand, Bowling Green Studies in Applied Philosophy, no. 2. Bowling Green: Applied Philosophy Program.

Vermazen, Bruce. 1985. "Negative Acts." In Vermazen and Hintikka 1985.

Vermazen, Bruce, and Merrill B. Hintikka, eds. 1985. *Essays on Davidson: Actions and Events.* Oxford: Oxford University Press.

Warner, R., and R. Grandy, eds. 1986. *Philosophical Grounds of Rationality.* Oxford: Oxford University Press.

Wiggins, David. 1975–1976. "Deliberation and Practical Reason." *Aristotelian Society Proceedings* 76:29–51.

Wiggins, David. 1978–1979. "Weakness of Will, Commensurability, and the Objects of Deliberation and Desire." *Aristotelian Society Proceedings* 79:251–277.

Wiggins, David. 1985. "Claims of Need." In *Morality and Objectivity,* edited by T. Honderich. London: Routledge.

Wiggins, David. 1987. *Needs, Values, Truth.* Oxford: Blackwell.

Williams, Bernard. 1979. "Internal and External Reasons." In

218   *Rational Action,* edited by R. Harrison. Cambridge: Cambridge University Press. Reprinted in Williams 1981.

Williams, Bernard. 1981. *Moral Luck.* Cambridge: Cambridge University Press.

Williams, Bernard. 1985. *Ethics and the Limits of Philosophy.* Cambridge: Harvard University Press.

Williams, Bernard. 1989. "Internal Reasons and the Obscurity of Blame." *Logos* 10:1–11.

Wilson, George M. 1989. *The Intentionality of Human Action.* Stanford: Stanford University Press. •

Winch, Peter. 1972. *Ethics and Action.* London: Routledge and Kegan Paul.

Wittgenstein, Ludwig. 1953. *Philosophical Investigations.* New York: Macmillan.

Wolf, Susan. 1990. *Freedom within Reason.* New York: Oxford University Press.

Wollheim, Richard. 1984. *The Thread of Life.* Cambridge: Harvard University Press.

Woodfield, Andrew, ed. 1982. *Thought and Object: Essays on Intentionality.* Oxford: Oxford University Press.

Woodward, James, and Terence Horgan. 1985. "Folk Psychology Is Here to Stay." *Philosophical Review* 94:197–226.

Index